Scriptures to SUCCESS

Scriptures to Success

L. Lionel Kendrick

© 1983, 1993 L. Lionel Kendrick

All rights reserved. No part of this book may be reproduced in any form or by any means without permission in writing from the publisher, Deseret Book Company, P.O. Box 30178, Salt Lake City, Utah 84130. This work is not an official publication of The Church of Jesus Christ of Latter-day Saints. The views expressed herein are the responsibility of the author and do not necessarily represent the position of the Church or of Deseret Book Company.

Deseret Book is a registered trademark of Deseret Book Company.

First printing in 1983 by Randall Book Company.
Second printing in 1993 by Deseret Book Company.

ISBN 0–87579–825–X

Printed in the United States of America

10   9   8   7   6   5   4   3   2

ACKNOWLEDGMENTS

Special appreciation is given to Joel and Barbara Gillespie for their encouragement and suggestions in this project.

I would like to thank Susan Dale, who made a significant contribution in typing the manuscript and also Jim Dale for his valuable assistance.

DEDICATION

To my wife, Myrtis, who has lived the true principles of success found in the scriptures. Her life emulates success as a wife and mother. I love her and am grateful for her constant support. This book is dedicated to her.

TABLE OF CONTENTS

Acknowledgments................................... v
Dedication.. vi
Foreword.. ix
Introduction...................................... 1

STEP I   DECIDE
Chapter 1   Pursuit of Purpose 5
Chapter 2   Growing with Goals 9
Chapter 3   Challenge of Commitment............... 13

STEP II   BELIEVE
Chapter 4   Strengthening Self-Image.............. 18
Chapter 5   Attention to Attitude 27

STEP III   LEARN
Chapter 6   Preparation for Perfection............ 42
Chapter 7   Reaching Righteous Relationships 49

STEP IV   ACT
Chapter 8   Observance of Obedience............... 66
Chapter 9   Mastering Motivation.................. 70
Chapter 10   Will to Work 83

STEP V   ENDURE
Chapter 11   Answers About Adversity 88
Chapter 12   Personal Perseverance 98

FOREWORD

Jesus Christ was rejected by a people who claimed a mastery of the scriptures. To them he said: "Search the scriptures; for in them ye think ye have eternal life: and they are they which testify of me" (John 5:39). This passage has often been misunderstood. His was not a discourse on the blessings of scriptural study, but rather a rebuke to those who falsely supposed that their ability to quote scriptures assured them eternal life. For all their knowledge, those to whom the Savior spoke had missed the central point of the scriptural message, for they failed to recognize him as the long promised Messiah.

Revelation 1:3, which is part of John's preface to his great revelation received on the Isle of Patmos, reads: "Blessed is he that readeth, and they that hear the words of this prophecy, and keep those things which are written therein: for the time is at hand." In so writing, John was announcing that his work was to be considered scripture and that it was to be read by the saints on a par with the books of the Old Testament. Those who read it to the congregations of the saints would be blessed, he promised, as would those who faithfully listened to it being read. Throughout the centuries this led to the tradition of reading the Book of Revelation in various religious services, that reader and listener might accrue the promised blessings, though an understanding of the book had long been lost.

As scriptural history so amply attests, it is one thing to read and quote the scripture and entirely another to understand and live its injunctions. In his inspired translation of Revelation 1:3, Joseph Smith restored the word "understand" to the text. Thus the blessing promised by John, as originally intended, was limited to those who "understand" and "keep" the sayings of their prophet.

The profession of truth is never lacking among false religionists. They zealously read and quote scripture. What one fails to find in their theology is that understanding that demands advancement from "grace to grace" that they may, in due time, receive of the fullness of the Father (D&C 93:19-20). The primary strength of L. Lionel Kendrick's *Scriptures To Success* is the impelling desire to aid the reader in that spiritual quest and the specific suggestions as to how it can be done. The work is an appropriate and insightful union of *understanding* and *application* of gospel principles.

Joseph F. McConkie
Associate Professor of
Ancient Scripture
Brigham Young University

INTRODUCTION

The word "success" is rarely mentioned in the scriptures even though they are the source for real success. The Lord spoke to Joshua, giving him instructions that if followed, would make him infinitely successful. He gave Joshua both the principle and the promise concerning the scriptures as a source of success:

> This book of the law shall not depart out of thy mouth; but thou shalt meditate therein day and night, that thou mayest observe to do according to all that is written therein: for then thou shalt make thy way prosperous, and then thou shalt have good success. (Joshua 1:8.)

This powerful instruction is the foundation of a personal success system in mortality. The principles of success are found throughout the scriptures.

My professional pursuits have enabled me to review several hundred research studies and other sources relating to human behavior and the resolution of problems; however, I have found from my search of the scriptures that the answers to *all* of life's questions are found either in the scriptures or in the counsel of the Brethren. Elder Neal A. Maxwell so amply summarizes the scriptural roots of success as he states:

> ... many of the critical data about human nature are already available in the scriptures; these data do not need to be discovered but merely openly accepted and seriously applied. (Neal A. Maxwell, *The Smallest Part*, [Salt Lake City, Deseret Book Company], 1973, p. 5.)

Heavenly Father desires that each of us succeed and prosper during our probation. He has promised, "Do this thing which I have commanded you and you shall prosper ..." (D&C 9:13.). He has further promised that He "... will provide means whereby thou mayest accomplish the thing which I have commanded thee" (D&C 5:34). It is Satan who scorns success and fights to instill fear and failure in our lives.

I have personally searched the scriptures and other sources to give structure to the process of attaining success. To gain a conception of the commandments is a most spiritually rewarding experience. The results of my search form the design for this book which is divided into five steps to success. Within each section are chapters devoted to the principles of success. I have merged truths from the scriptures and other sources into one system. Since the Gospel embraces all truth and since the Savior has said "that all things unto me are spiritual" (D&C 29:34), this task has been spiritually motivated.

STEP I:
Decide

"It does not take much strength to do things, but it takes a great strength to decide on what to do." (Elbert Hubbard)

We have been given the capacity to choose and the freedom to function, which is at the heart of the plan of salvation. It was this principle that separated the Savior from Satan. The battle from the beginning will be the fight to the finish for the choices that we make in mortality.

Heavenly Father expects us to exercise control of our choices. Indecision is not a Godly characteristic. When we leave our choices to chance, Satan attempts to gain control. Procrastination is a tool of the adversary with which he attempts to delay us into destruction rather than have us decide our divine destiny. Elijah was frustrated with his people as they idled in indecision. He fervently posed the question, "How long halt ye between two opinions?" (I Kings 18:21). Joshua faced a similar dilemma as he challenged his people to "choose you this day whom ye will serve" (Joshua 24:15).

It is a fundamental principle that for every choice we make, there is a consequence which may be very pleasurable or very painful, but always present. Each of our choices will be choices of "good or evil" (Alma 13:3) and will gain us the consequences of eternal "life or death" (Helaman 14:31).

The first step in any success is to make a decision. We must decide what is important in life (our purpose), what we want to achieve (our goals), and then we must decide to do all that is necessary to succeed (our commitment). I challenge you to decide this day to pursue perfection. Once the decision is made, you are on the way to greater success.

Pursuit of Purpose   1

It is important to prayerfully ponder our purpose in life. Without discovering our divine destiny we tend to become discouraged. It is important to realize who we are, to see the value of increasing our vision, to look at our values, and then to plan our priorities.

Who Am I?

There are some universal answers to this question that may add to our feeling of self-worth.

1. I Am Unique

    Of all the spirits who have been born, who now live, or who will ever live on earth, no two are exactly alike. Not even identical twins are duplicates. That makes each of us special, and that is why we enjoy and desire being treated as special. This desire is divine and had its beginning at our celestial birth. The deprivation of this desire will cause us to develop feelings of depression and ultimate despair.

2. I Have Infinite Possibilities

    Our ultimate possibilities had their inception in our spiritual conception. We toiled with our talents in the premortal existence and brought with us the seeds of our ultimate success.

    We have the talents necessary to gain Godhood. Our task is to discover, cultivate, and multiply these talents. The Savior provides the light for their discovery, the time to test them, and the opportunities to overcome the opposition. Satan attempts to dim our vision of this possibility of Godhood. He helps us to discover deceptive ways to destroy our talents and to prevent our progression. Many of us behave like the unwise steward when he responded, "I was afraid, and went and hid thy talent" (Matthew 25:25), thus limiting our ultimate possibilities.

3. I Am A Child of God

The impact of this single eternal truth is enough to stimulate the search for success. This is precisely why we are so important and is the reason some even feel the need to fanaticize this feeling of importance. In the premortal we were nurtured by divine parents, who, with a perfect love, made us feel important and gave us every reason to seek that feeling in mortality.

There should be no doubt as to our eternal lineage. In the planning councils of Heaven, Father said, "Let us make man in our own image, after our likeness" (Genesis 1:26). Joshua spoke of our royal lineage as he explained that we are sons of God (see 1 John 3:2). Paul, preaching to the Athenians, said, "we are also his offspring" (Acts 17:28).

Our challenge is to act upon this great truth and not be torn by the turmoil of the times. If we so live, we may be close to our eternal parents and feel their presence still sending messages of counsel and comfort. We must remember our divine destiny and our royal relationship with Heavenly Father.

Value of Vision

The process of deciding demands that we expand our

vision and stretch our sights in order to experience success. In Proverbs we find the counsel, "Where there is no vision the people perish" (Proverbs 29:18). This admonition not only applies to a world without a prophet, but it is also critical counsel for each of us personally.

> Where there is no vision,
>   there is no challenge.
> Where there is no challenge,
>   there is no growth,
> Where there is no growth,
>   there is no life.
> Where there is no life,
>   there is only death.
>   —Lionel Kendrick

Satan is the master of mediocrity, which is the alternative to vision. He is a master of this method. Nephi was aware of this and warned us, "And others will he pacify, and lull them away into carnal security, that they will say: All is well in Zion; yea, Zion prospereth, all is well—and thus the devil cheateth their souls, and leadeth them carefully down to hell" (2 Nephi 28:21).

Viewing Values

Values are the foundation of our character and of our confidence. A person who does not know what he stands for or what he should stand for, will never enjoy true happiness and success.

Some values are eternal in nature. These should never be compromised or changed. They should be based upon obeying the commandments and the counsel of God. Other values are transient in nature and change as we mature. The Apostle Paul described these when he said, "When I was a child, I spake as a child, I understood as a child, I thought as a child; but when I became a man, I put away childish things" (1 Corinthians 13:11).

Satan attempts to lead us into situations where we will

not stand for our values. Paul warned, "Beware lest any man spoil you through philosophy and vain deceit, after the traditions of men, after the rudiments of the world, and not after Christ" (Colossians 2:8). The pseudo philosophies and tried traditions of men today strike at the roots of spiritual value systems. Their vain voices echo the sentiments of Satan saying, "There are no absolutes in values; if it feels good, go with it." Hypocrisy can be heard in their voices as they attempt to impose their values on parents proposing that they have no right to teach or to transmit parental values on children.

It is often rewarding to regularly review our values that our purpose may be clear. A view of our present values may be gained by focusing on the following:

1. Think of the person of whom we are most fond. List five characteristics of this person that we highly value. In this manner we may discover what values we place importance on.
2. Think of the person of whom we are the least fond. List five undesirable characteristics of this person. These items will also give us a view of our values. We hold these things in low esteem in our lives and in the lives of others. The opposite of these traits would be of high value to us.

Planning Priorities

Once we decide what is of high value, the next step is to set priorities. Based upon our values, we can now develop a list of things in order of their importance to us at this time. These priorities should be reviewed on a regular basis.

Growing with Goals 2

After we ponder our purpose in life, and have identified our priorities, it is important that we set goals. A goal is nothing more than that which we intend to attain, but it is essential to our success.

In setting our personal goals we should always be influenced by our eternal goals and remember the real purposes for which we are on earth, that is: to gain a body, to gain experiences, and to prove ourselves.

The Savior summarized His goals when he said, "For behold, this is my work and my glory—to bring to pass the immortality and eternal life of man" (Moses 1:39). It was evident that the Apostle Paul also set specific goals as he expressed, "I press toward the mark [goal] for the prize of the high calling of God in Christ Jesus" (Philippians 3:14).

President Spencer W. Kimball expressed his feelings concerning the setting of goals as he said, "We do believe in setting goals . . . Our most important goal is to bring the gospel to all people . . ." (President Spencer W. Kimball, Regional Representative Seminar, October 14, 1973.)

Guidelines for Goals

A system for goal setting should be simple if it is to be successful. Certain guidelines should be considered in setting goals:

    1. Goals should be personal

           Personally set goals will stimulate internal

motivation, thus increasing the possibility for successful performance. That which we personally desire to do generates greater energy.

2. Goals should be written

    A written goal enables us to visualize as well as verbalize our desires. The process of written communication helps us to crystalize our thinking.

3. Goals should be specific

    There is a common tendency to be vague and general in setting goals. Vagueness reduces the vividness and the value of what we are attempting to accomplish.

4. Goals should be measurable

    If we are to maximize our motivation to reach a goal, it should be measurable. For example, we should not set a goal to read the scriptures. This is general in nature. It would be much more effective to set a goal to read a certain number of pages in the scriptures.

5. Goals should have a deadline for completion

    Without a deadline we will have a tendency to delay. Deadlines give us a point at which we can come to closure on the goal. Target dates for completion will increase our effort.

6. Goals should be realistic, but challenging

    There are few unrealistic goals, just unrealistic deadlines. Given enough time, we can accomplish much. Without a challenge, a goal will not be stimulating or exciting to achieve. Stretching is vital to success. President Spencer W. Kimball has counseled that we should make no small plans because they have no magic to stir men's souls.

7. Goals should be true to one's value system

    There should be no conflict in our goals and

values. If the pursuit of a specific goal prevents us from achieving other goals, such as having a successful family life or completing church assignments, then we should have reservations as to the importance of that goal.

8. Goals should be flexible

    Situations will occur when we may want to substitute one goal for another. When positive proposals do present themselves, flexibility is important. General Authorities have been deeply involved in their professional pursuits when their calls came and changed their goals in a significant way.

9. Goals should be positive

    We should avoid setting negative goals where possible. Instead of setting a goal to not lose our temper, we should set a goal to keep our emotions in control.

10. Goals should be monitored

    A serious mistake is to have a well-developed written goal that rarely gets reviewed. To be effective, progress should be monitored.

CHALLENGES
1. Set goals using the above guidelines.
2. Review goals daily.

Goal Achievement Plan

Once goals have been selected and written, an action plan should be developed. We do not "do" goals, we "do" actions. The following "Goal Achievement Plan" may be helpful in developing an action plan. This plan should be reviewed on a daily basis.

GOAL ACHIEVEMENT PLAN

GOAL

COMMITMENT

I hereby commit that **I will** achieve the above goal by taking the following actions:

ACTIONS

Challenge of Commitment 3

Once we have set goals, it is critical that we make a strong commitment to act. A commitment is a promise made to ourself or to others.

Commitments are not unique to this mortal realm; they were part of the celestial councils. We stood, and with a sustaining voice and hand, sealed our support for the plan of salvation. The Lord has always asked for commitments from His children. He counsels us to "commit thy way unto the Lord; trust also in him; and he shall bring it to pass" (Psalms 37:5). The commitments that we make to the Lord are in the form of covenants.

Importance

There is great power in a promise to perform. When the mind, spirit and body are sealed in a singleness of purpose, we gain great strength in our performance. A commitment is a form of burning our bridges behind us once we have decided the direction that we should go. It helps us to focus on our goal rather than its alternative. The Savior warned of wrong-way wandering when He said, "No man, having put his hand to the plough, and looking back, is fit for the kingdom of God" (Luke 9:62).

We often leave ourselves an escape. When faced with making a commitment, we sometimes respond with cautious communications such as "If," "I'll try," "Maybe," "I can't," or "I'm not sure." These are not communications of commitment, but expressions of comfortable convenience. The language of commitment is simple and is stated in two words, "I will."

Commitment is sometimes communicated by means of action. When the Savior was walking by the Sea of Galilee, He issued a divine call to Peter and Andrew as He said to them, "Follow me and I will make you fishers of men" (Matthew 4:19). It is recorded that their response was one without reservation as "They straightway left their nets and followed him" (Matthew 4:20). The same response to the call was made by each of the Twelve. There was no delay, doubt, or need for further discussion. They simply made a decision and a commitment for a life of service and sacrifice.

If we are to be successful, we must also be willing to make a definite commitment to accomplish whatever we have decided to do and have set in the form of goals. From the point of our decision we too must not delay or doubt. Commitment is not just important, but it is critical to success.

Examples

There are many great examples of commitment in the scriptures. Many have shown the strength of their character as they made commitments to the cause.

The Savior's entire earthly life was one of commitment. He submitted Himself to the will of His Father. ". . . I came into the world to do the will of my Father, because my Father sent me" (3 Nephi 27:13).

Lehi gave his son Nephi the very difficult assignment to go to the house of Laban and obtain the records and bring them to him in the wilderness. Nephi realized that he would have little support from his brothers, as they had already begun to murmur and complain about how difficult this assignment would be. Nephi was not shaken in his confidence, and he made a commitment to his father as he said, "*I will* go and do the things which the Lord hath commanded, for I know that the Lord giveth no commandments unto the children of men, save he shall prepare a way for them that they may accomplish the thing which he commandeth them" (1 Nephi 3:7).

After attempting and failing to achieve his assignment, Nephi, in the face of this failure, renewed his commitment as he resolved ". . . As the Lord liveth, and as we live, we *will not* go down unto our father in the wilderness until we have accomplished the thing which the Lord hath commanded us" (1 Nephi 3:15).

This level of commitment brings celestial consequences, and develops courage and character in each of us. Commitment is a critical principle of success.

STEP II:
Believe

"They conquer who believe they can."
(Emerson)

After we have declared our decisions, have given our goals, and communicated our commitment, then comes the need for a burning belief that we can accomplish that which we have determined to do. True success can come only to those who have a foundation of faith in the Lord (see D&C 20:29), in the gospel (see Ether 4:18), and in themselves (see Romans 10:9).

We learned faith at the feet of Heavenly Father in the preexistence. It would be foolish to think that He would send us here to seek exaltation and to return to Him without having faith. He taught us trust to take into mortality that we might be true to the things that would bring us home again. We now must "walk by faith, not by sight" (II Corinthians 5:7).

The Lord has given a powerful promise to those who exercise faith. He promised that "all things are possible to him that believeth" (Mark 9:23), but for those who fail to believe, He has said, "he that believeth not shall be damned"

(D&C 68:9). Success is severely slowed for those who cannot conceive this counsel of the Savior.

This belief has both a spiritual and intellectual base. We must do all that we can to strengthen our self-image and to give proper attention to our attitudes if we are to be succesful both spiritually and temporally.

Strengthening Self-Image 4

At birth the veil did not dim our need for a feeling of self-worth. Our desire to succeed, to be self-reliant, and to be happy was given to us by our spiritual parents. It was their desire that we would always be aware of these celestial characteristics. The development of love, trust, faith, and self-motivation in their pure childlike form is essential for our return to the presence of our heavenly parents. As He blessed the little children, the Savior counseled "Whosoever shall not receive the Kingdom of God as a little child, he shall not enter therein" (Mark 10:15).

Probation is our time of preparation to continue to develop these childlike characteristics. The experiences of this life and our responses to them will determine the direction and the degree of our development.

Early in this process, demonstrable differences in each of us begin to be discerned. Some become achievers, while others descend to levels of disappointment and depression. The real differences may be determined by the self-image of the individuals.

The concept of self-image and self-esteem are often used synonymously because they are so closely linked. These two concepts of self are important to our success. Self-image is a mental picture that we have of ourself, while self-esteem is a feeling of our worth. This perception and associated feelings have a profound effect upon our performance. It may be described as the degree to which we appreciate and accept ourselves and the degree of confidence, comfort, and control we possess.

PERSONAL PERCEPTION

Much of our success is dependent upon our self-perception. Seneca once wrote "Know thyself, this is the great object." Self-knowledge is a step to self-acceptance and self-accomplishment. The following Perception Profile may be helpful in assessing our level of self-esteem. Indicate the degree of response using this scale:

1 = Always
2 = Frequently
3 = Half time
4 = Infrequently
5 = Never

____I am shy
____I avoid people
____I am defensive
____I am afraid to speak up
____I am suspicious of others
____I fear failure
____I give up easily
____I feel inadequate

____I am boastful
____I am rebellious
____I criticize others
____I blame others
____I resent authority
____I hate criticism
____I procrastinate
____I feel unhappy

High = 64-80   Average = 33-63   Low = 16-32

FOUNDATIONS

In order to more fully understand ourselves, our attitudes, and our actions, it may be helpful to gain a greater knowledge of how our self-image functions.

Performance

Perception and performance are highly related. We are not able to perform independently of the way we see and feel about ourselves. This is significant to our success as our performance will be consistent with our perceptions.

When we perform above or below our preconceived

comfort zone, we will quickly return to our preconceived performance level. Performance outside our comfort zone creates discomfort or dissonance. Our body immediately sends us feedback signals such as tenseness, increased breathing and heart rates, and in some cases, anxiety.

This principle of performance is applied in every phase of our lives. A missionary can be no more effective than he sees himself. If his image is low, and he has the attitude that he cannot make the necessary life-style adjustments, he will begin to act and feel as he perceives himself. He will begin to procrastinate, to feel sorry for himself and to bend and break mission rules while feeling perfectly justified in doing so. Satan suddenly swamps him in self-pity and self-delusion. His concentration starts to focus on reaching the end of the day rather than reaching people in the proselyting process. His love for the Savior becomes lost in his lack of self-image.

David, the young shepherd boy, was an example of one who had a strong self-image and a high perception of his performance. When the Philistine giant, Goliath, defied the army of Israel to send a man to fight, they were afraid. It was said that ". . . when they saw the man, [they] fled from him, and were sore afraid" (1 Samuel 17:24). Young David had no fear but instead he had great faith in the Lord. As he approached Goliath to engage him in combat, he said, "Thou comest to me with a sword, and with a spear, and with a shield: but I come to thee in the name of the Lord of hosts, the God of the armies of Israel, whom thou hast defied. This day the Lord will deliver thee into mine hand; and I will smite thee . . ." (1 Samuel 17:45-46.) David not only had a powerful perception of his potential, but also a deep faith in the Lord which he boldly communicated with confidence to Goliath.

When Israel was in bondage to the Midianites, the people cried to the Lord for help. An angel appeared to Gideon and told him that he would be responsible to save Israel. Gideon's response was at this point not one of confidence as was David's. Gideon said to the angel, ". . . my family is poor in Manasseh, and I am the least of my father's house" (Judges 6:15). He was saying that he was the least son in one of the least families in a lesser tribe of Israel. The Lord promised Gideon, "Surely I will be with thee. . ." (Judges 6:16). This immediately changed Gideon's perception and with an army reduced to 300, he was successful against great odds in saving Israel.

The Apostle Paul counseled, "Let every man be fully persuaded in his own mind" (Romans 14:5). We must develop a healthy image of ourselves in our own minds. Circumstances may change, but what does not change is our capacity to control our actions and feelings. To believe otherwise would be to deny the great principle of free agency.

Brain

The brain has often been compared with a computer. While this comparison may be helpful in furthering our understanding, we must always remember that the brain has divine dimensions and has no duplicates. Its capacity to choose and to control its own directions and ultimate destiny under the influence of the Spirit, has no comparison with the computer.

The fifteen billion cells of the brain are capable of a million chemical responses, and they provide us with the means of perceiving, storing, processing, and recalling the experiences that we gain during our earthly as well as our eternal existence. It is estimated that in a lifetime the brain can store a million billion bits of information.

Thinking

The mind is never blank, even though we may feel that it fails us at times. It is full of thoughts and active at all times. It can process in excess of 1,400 thoughts per minute, which is ten times the rate of speaking. This difference is the reason our attention span is sometimes short; we become bored because we can think faster than input is received. Our active mind wanders, searching for activity. Therefore, an idle mind does become the devil's workshop.

Self-Talk

About ninety percent of our communication takes place silently in our own minds. We continuously send ourselves mental messages, and it is from these concealed communications that we often draw our conclusions. If we consistently send ourselves negative messages, we may be convinced by these concepts. Many spirits tend to sag from a saturation of self-sent sadness.

CREATING

Self-image once formed is not final; it can be changed. From our weaknesses can come great strengths. The process of creating a more positive self-image is three-fold. It involves an understanding of our weaknesses, a perception of our potential, and an application of true techniques to strengthen our image.

Weaknesses

A great limitation for some is the weaknesses that we possess. We may spend more time worrying about our weaknesses rather than focusing on our strengths. Heavenly Father has provided each of us with our share of weaknesses, but He did so for a proper purpose. He said, "I give unto men weakness that they may be humble" (Ether 12:27). He gives us a positive way to manage them along with a promise that "if they [we] humble themselves before me, and have faith in men, then will I make weak things become strong unto them" (Ether 12:27).

Weaknesses can work for our good if we recognize their divine purpose, be humbled but not humiliated by them, and if we express faith in Heavenly Father rather than fear of our frailties.

Potential

Psychologists have indicated that the average person functions at less than ten percent of their potential. We must remember that our potential is relative rather than rigid. As we develop our talents, our ultimate potential becomes greater.

During our pre-earth life we toiled with our talents and brought them with us to continue their development in our earthly experience. Some arrived in this life with many talents while others came with few. The reason for this is dimmed by the veil, but this should have no effect on achievements in this life.

With His perfect perception, the Savior has counseled "For of him unto whom much is given much is required; (D&C 82:3, Luke 12:48). His counsel is clear "that every man may improve upon his talents, that every man may gain other talents, yea, even an hundred fold" (D&C 82:18). If we accept this sacred challenge, we will more clearly conceive our ultimate potential, and then one day we can receive the marvelous feedback that the faithful servant in the parable of the talents received, when the Savior said, "Well done thou good and faithful servant: thou hast been faithful over a few things, I will make thee ruler over many things: enter thou into thy joy of the Lord" (Matthew 25:21).

What are we doing with our talents and the potential that we possess? Are we neglecting them, wasting them, using them, or increasing them? It may be helpful to make a list of our strengths. We may ask a friend to list strengths that he sees in us. We should then review our strengths in relation to the above questions.

Techniques

The following techniques are designed to help create a

more positive self-image. These techniques are natural and are the precise means by which our self-image is formed in the first place. New techniques are not necessary; we must simply control and utilize these techniques in a more positive manner. There are three basic sources from which we develop a self-image: thoughts, images, and feelings.

1. Thoughts

Our thoughts tend to control our self-concept. We must be careful of what we communicate to ourselves. The process that we use to control these communications is called *verbalization*. It involves controlling our self-talk, what we read, what we listen to, and what we speak.

Self-talk, the silent communication of mental messages, must be carefully controlled. We should consistently send ourselves positive communications even when our performance may not so indicate. When mistakes are made, there is no point in a personal put-down. With repetition these mental messages are recorded in the subconscience where they are accepted as reality. This process should by no means minimize our perception of unrighteous activity. When we minimize sin, we diminish our conscience, thus restricting our ability to repent.

Careful consideration should be given to what we *read*, as it too will be recorded in the recesses of the mind. This information can be recalled, and it may haunt, hurt, and hinder our eternal quest. There is great importance in the admonition "seek ye out of the best books words of wisdom" (D&C 88:118). The search for truth should start in the scriptures. We should read those things which inspire and instruct our spirit.

That which we *listen* to influences our thoughts and becomes a lasting part of our lives. Our self-image will be strengthened by listening to inspirational talks, tapes, conversations, and music.

Our own *verbal conversations* should be reviewed for their positive and uplifting tones. Our verbalizations are a reflection of our thoughts and feelings.

2. Images

Early in life we learned a technique called *visualization*. We may have spent much time creating images of life as we would like it to be. We dreamed dreams and lived them out in the creations of our mind. This natural process can be most positive unless we spend too much time in our dream world and too little time in reality.

With this great creative power of visualization, we can create experiences that have never existed. It can take us through time and space to exciting places.

These positive points about visualization do have their potential problems. Satan attempts to use this power to channel our thoughts on actions that are degrading, carnal, and lustful in nature. The Savior gives clear counsel on this matter when He said, "Whosoever looketh on a woman to lust after her hath committed adultery with her already in his heart" (Matthew 5:28, see also D&C 63:16). "For out of the heart proceed evil thoughts, murders, adulteries, fornications, thefts, false witness, blasphemies" (Matthew 15:19).

The positive uses of visualization are most valuable in strengthening our self-image. We should see success before seeking it. Our focus should be on success rather than failure.

3. Feelings

Emotional feelings, both pleasurable and painful, are stored in the limbic system of the brain. They are recorded just as our thoughts and images are recorded for later review.

We have the ability to replay any emotional feeling that we have experienced. It is strengthening to our self-image to replay and briefly review these positive feelings from our past.

Some years ago a young graduate student shared an experience that is an example of the application of each of the above techniques. She gained strength even in he face of adversity. One morning at breakfast her twenty-five-year-old husband suddenly died of a heart attack. This was a most traumatic experience in her life. She later took one room in her house and called it her "ego" room. In it she placed a collection of many of the most positive things that she had experienced in her life. There were press clippings, pictures, awards, letters, report cards and other cherished possessions. As needed, she would close the door and sit in a recliner and review her positive past, mentally give herself a pep talk, and visualize that which she wanted in the future.

Self-image is indeed significant to our success. As we better understand how it is formed, how it functions, and how it can be changed, we are able to increase our faith in ourselves and in others. We will also be able to have greater control of both our perceptions and our performances.

Attention to Attitude 5

Our basic belief in self is based on the strength of our self-image and is closely related to the attention we give to our attitudes. The answer to our actions can be found in the attitudes we attain. This association should be given close attention.

CONCEPTS

Attitudes are not without their foundation. Our beliefs are born of our thoughts. This concept is but a part of a general framework in which we function.

Levels of Functioning

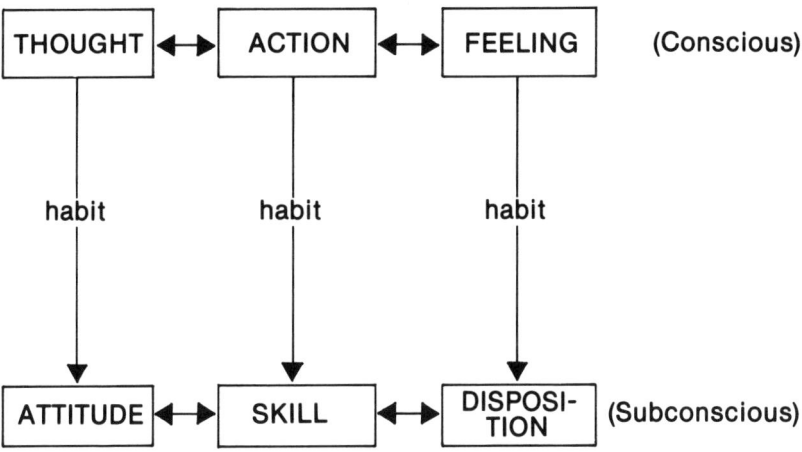

If we properly understand this framework and apply its principles, we will discover some interesting truths that affect our life. The manner in which we function on both the conscious and subconscious level determines our destiny.

1. Conscious Level

    Thoughts, actions and feelings are very much interrelated. As we change one we also stimulate change in the others. For example, if we feel depressed, we will tend to think and act in a depressed manner.

    The Apostle Paul taught this principle of interrelationship to the Corinthian saints when he said, "God hath tempered the body together. . . That there should be no schism in the body; but that the members should have the same care one for another. And whether one member suffer, all the members suffer with it; or one member be honoured, all the members rejoice with it." (I Corinthians 12:24-26.)

2. Subconscious Level

    Once we repeat a thought, action, or feeling enough, it is recorded in the subconscious. Here it becomes part of our automatic activity in the form of habits, no longer needing conscious stimulus to sustain it.

Thoughts

Our thoughts are the source of our constant struggle with Satan. Certain concepts about thoughts have eternal consequences.

1. Our thoughts control us

    William James, a noted psychologist, made the discovery that "the thought precedes the action." This was not a new discovery as the world believed it to be; it was only a new disclosure of an eternal discovery found in Proverbs: "For as he thinketh in his heart, so is he" (Proverbs 23:7). Plato knew this eternal truth when he counseled, "Take control of your thoughts, you can do with them what you want." Marcus Aurelius, that great Roman ruler and philosopher, said, "Our life is what our thoughts make it." James Allen reinforced this concept as he warned, "You are today where your thoughts have brought you; you will be tomorrow where your thoughts take you." Milton, in *Paradise Lost,* observed, "The mind is its own place and in itself can make a heaven of hell or a hell of heaven."

2. The Lord knows our thoughts

   The veil does not screen the vision of His children from the Lord. His vision is celestially clear, with full perception of our purity and of our performance. His vision transcends matter and goes to the innermost parts of our intelligence in our spirit substance. He spoke to Ezekiel with a warning: "I know the things that come into your mind, every one of them" (Ezekiel 11:5). He issued the same warning to Isaiah concerning his people. "For I know their works and their thoughts" (Isaiah 66:18). Alma was aware of this principle as he taught "he looketh down upon all the children of men; and he knows all the thoughts and intents of the heart" (Alma 18:32). This power is reserved for the members of the Godhead. ". . . there is none else save God that knowest thy thoughts and the intents of thy heart" (D&C 6:16).

3. Thoughts attract their kind

   Thoughts neurologically attract similar thoughts. A person may move from a moment of disappointment to discouragement and even to depression. Worry can lead to wrong doing. This principle was explained by the Savior when He said,

"For intelligence cleaveth unto intelligence; wisdom receiveth wisdom; truth embraceth truth; virtue loveth virtue; light cleaveth unto light" (D&C 88: 40). President McKay frequently quoted the following:

We sow our thoughts and we reap our actions;
We sow our actions and we reap our habits;
We sow our habits and we reap our character;
We sow our character and we reap our destiny.
(C.A. Hall, *The Home Book of Quotations,* [New York: Dodd, Mead and Company], 1935, p. 845.)

Attitudes

Attitudes are simply habits of thoughts. The quality of our thoughts will determine the quality of our attitudes. Negative attitudes drain our energy, canker our spirit, and eat away at our motivation and peace of mind. Positive attitudes have the reverse effect. They allow the body and spirit to perform together resulting in increased performance, peace of mind, and they add to our longevity.

Actions

Thoughts precede actions; therefore, if we control the thought, we control the action. It is no wonder that Satan challenges the control center for our thoughts and actions. In his drive for the destruction of souls, he discovered the device that could lead them into destruction.

Actions are essential for eternal achievement. The Savior said, "Why call ye me, Lord, Lord, and do not the things which I say?" (Luke 6:46). The warning is very clear that "Not everyone that saith unto me, Lord, Lord shall enter into the kingdom of heaven; but he that *doeth* the will of my Father" (Matthew 7:21).

Skill

Actions which are repeated become habits of skill. As

skill develops, performance is increased. We are admonished to continually pray, study the scriptures, and attend meetings. These and other actions build skills for Godhood.

Feelings

Our feelings follow our thoughts and actions. This association has been from the beginning. Peter pointed to this principle when he said, "For he that will love life, and see good days, let him refrain his tongue from evil, and his lips that they speak no guile" (1 Peter 3:10).

Good days depend upon good deeds. This enables us to be delivered from feelings of depression for "if ye sow good ye shall also reap good for your reward" (D&C 6:33). The scriptures warn that "the rebellious shall be pierced with much sorrow" (D&C 1:3). "There is no peace, saith my God, to the wicked" (Isaiah 57:21), "to be spiritually minded is life and peace" (Romans 8:6).

Disposition

As we continue to feel certain feelings for periods of time, we develop a habit of feeling called a disposition. We can develop a disposition that is characteristically sweet or characteristically sour, depending upon our feelings. Our countenance is controlled by the frequency of our feelings.

Scriptural Example

One of the great examples in the scriptures of the contrast of attitudes as they relate to thoughts, actions, and feelings, is seen in the contrast between Nephi and his brother Laman. Their lives are an example of the contrast between the positive and negative with the ultimate contrasting consequences.

As they departed from their home and possessions in Jerusalem, their responses were quite different to this requested departure: Nephi's attitude was quite evident in his expression that he had "great desires to know of the mysteries of God . . ." (1 Nephi 2:16). He acted upon his great desire as he "did cry unto the Lord. . ." (1 Nephi 2:16). As a result of his prayerful petition to the Lord, his prayer was answered, and he experienced a softened heart (1 Nephi 2:16). On this same occasion Laman's response was more rebellious than righteous. Instead of a desire to know the will of the Lord, Laman expressed an attitude of doubt. He did not believe that Lehi had received a revelation but that he had led them into the wilderness "because of the foolish imaginations of his heart" (1 Nephi 2:11). As a result of this doubtful attitude, his actions were also affected, and he and Lemuel "did murmur against their father . . ." (1 Nephi 2:12). Their feelings toward Lehi were hardened. Nephi described the feelings of his brother as being "like unto the Jews, who were at Jerusalem, who sought to take away the life of my father" (1 Nephi 2:13).

Lehi received instructions from the Lord to send his sons back to Jerusalem to secure the records from the house of Laban. Nephi expressed an attitude of willingness when he was instructed of his father. He recognized that the request of his father was ". . . a commandment of the Lord" (1 Nephi 3:5) and therefore was willing to respond to the request. He proceeded to act by making a sacred commitment to "do the things which the Lord hath commanded . . ." (1 Nephi 3:7). The feeling that came over him was one of complete confidence as he said, "I know that the Lord giveth no commandments unto the children of men, save he shall prepare a way for them that they may accomplish the thing which he commandeth them" (1 Nephi 3:7). As usual, the response of Laman was quite opposite for he displayed an attitude of indifference to the request of his father. He complained, "saying it is a hard thing . . ." (1 Nephi 3:5). The feeling of resistance and resentment are evident in the tone of his response.

Nephi and his brothers were engaged in quite a struggle in Jerusalem as they attempted to secure the sacred records.

The true character of the two brothers was once again revealed as they responded to this stressful situation. In the face of open rebellion by his brothers, Nephi exhibited an attitude of determination to do that which they were sent to do. He recommitted himself to the challenge and said, "we will not go down unto our father in the wilderness until we have accomplished the thing which the Lord hath commanded us" (1 Nephi 3:15). His feeling of confidence was not shattered, but to the contrary it increased. Laman's attitude was one of rebellion as he was ready to "return unto his father in the wilderness" (1 Nephi 3:14). He applied peer pressure on his brothers. Nephi described the feelings of his brother when he said that Laman "was angry with me, and also with my father . . ." (1 Nephi 3:28).

As the family of Lehi was traveling in the wilderness, they became very fatigued and began to suffer due to a great need for food. Nephi attempted to slay animals for the food they so desperately needed. In the process he broke his bow and returned to his family with no food. Nephi, while disappointed, still maintained an attitude of faith in his ability to still secure food. He immediately began to act and made another bow out of a straight stick (see 1 Nephi 16:23). He must have felt a great sense of satisfaction in his accomplishment. Laman's attitude was one of defeat, and he turned once again to "murmur exceedingly. . ." (1 Nephi 16:20), even murmuring against the Lord. He began to feel "exceeding sorrowful . . ." (1 Nephi 16:20) and spent time in self-pity.

When the Lord gave the commandment to build a ship to cross the waters, Nephi responded with a spirit of optimism. He immediately began to discuss the details of the project with the Lord. (See 1 Nephi 17:9.) He was obedient to the instructions that he received and began the work of constructing the ship. Nephi, who was always positive, felt perhaps for the first time negative feelings concerning his brothers. He said that he was "exceeding sorrowful because of the hardness of their hearts. . ." (1 Nephi 17:19). Laman's attitude was one of defeat, and he refused to work on the project. He felt happy that Nephi, with little help, was experiencing difficulty in constructing the ship. He delighted to see his righteous brother suffer. (See 1 Nephi 17:19.)

This contrast was consistent and was evident on both the conscious and subconscious levels of functioning. Nephi and Laman, although brothers, had contrasting thoughts, attitudes, actions, skills, feelings, and dispositions. Nephi was extremely positive and as a result was most successful and received the blessings of the Lord. Laman was most negative and experienced failure in much of his life. The blessings of the Lord were not with him.

CONDITIONING

There are many things in life that condition our attitudes. The brain is like a video recorder and is sensitive to and stores what we perceive. This data is stored for the future and can be a source of strength or a source of strain. Every thought that we think, and all feelings, experiences, movements, words, and images formed, are stored for our self-development or our damnation.

Approximately 250 billion bits of information is stored over our lifetime. The storage is at the subconscious level. We could not handle a conscious view of this vast information at one time. Some things are temporary and have no long-term value; these are perceived for the present and are not stored for the future.

We are in charge of the camera and control the projector to replay what we relish. The film is fast, and the focus is fierce. The film that is not erased by repentance will be taken into eternity, where it will be reviewed with vividness for all to view. It has been said that "their iniquities shall be spoken upon the housetops, and their secret acts shall be revealed" (D&C 1:3). Elder Joseph Fielding Smith gave his assessment as to how this would take place when he said: "Now I have in mind that we will be judged according to our works, and that it will be shown as on a screen, just as we watch television, and our acts will appear to us just as they were in life..." (*The Instructor,* June 1967, p. 219.)

The brain receives positive and negative input in two major ways: impact and spaced repetition.

1. Impact

    Traumatic experiences make an instant impact and are driven to the subconscious and are deeply imprinted upon the brain. These startling experiences have a lasting effect on our attitudes, actions, and emotions.

    We can probably recall the occasion when we heard that President John F. Kennedy had been assassinated. This event was not only a national social shock, but also a deeply felt personal shock. This was the first time that a President of the United States had been assassinated during our lifetime. As a result of the suddenness and the shock of the experience, our recall of the details and of our response to them is probably still crystal clear.

2. Repetition

    The most common input that we receive comes from spaced repetition. When things are repeated several times, they are recorded for future recall. We must be most cautious of what we receive and repeat through this means. It is through this method that we develop most of our knowledge, habits, and attitudes.

Negative Input

The influence of negative input will depress our thoughts, actions, and feelings. It causes a heaviness to occur, which results in tired and drained feelings. The feeling of depression is a feeling of heaviness and is commonly referred to as a "heavy heart." The Savior used this description when He said, "Come unto me, all ye that labour and are heavy laden, and I will give you rest" (Matthew 11:28).

Much of what we read and hear is negative. And if the input from our environment is basically negative, it will have negative effect on the way we think, act, and feel. We must be aware of the input that we receive through the music we listen to, the television programs that we watch, the pornography that we are exposed to, and the communication that we hear.

> *Music.* Many of the most popular records and tapes that are at the top of the rating charts have words, messages, beats, and tones that are negative and are degrading and depressing to the spirit. We should be careful what we program the mind.
>
> *Television.* Soap operas and many prime time shows program the mind with thoughts, images, and feelings that are not acceptable to the Savior. This input can have a negative impact on our value system. After repeated viewing of scenes with low and unacceptable standards, the shock may soon wear off, and in time they may even seem acceptable. This is Satan's subtle strategy to strip us of our sacred values and to make sin seem evermore satisfying.
>
> *Pornography.* This is one of the most profound procedures used by the adversary to program us with precepts that violate sacred principles. If we take part in pornographic programming, we are inviting the influence of Satan into our lives. The invitation is easily given, but the departure of this influence will be most difficult. A contaminated mind is hard to clean.
>
> *Communications.* Listening to negative communications is damaging to our self-image. We will receive our daily share of negative input in many forms. We must avoid, where possible, being a part of this depressing dialogue regardless of its form.

Positive Input

This type of input lifts the spirits and soothes the soul. It stimulates thoughts, actions and feelings that are wholesome and worthy of acceptance. This input can also be in the form of what we read, what we see, and what we listen to by way of conversations and music. These should be well chosen for their quality, positive tones and for the principles that they teach.

COUNSEL

Much wise counsel has been given in the scriptures concerning our thoughts, our attitudes, and our outlook in life. This counsel is not only wise, but it is most practical as it can be applied in every phase of our lives. If we will follow this counsel, we will not only be more successful, but we will also receive greater satisfaction in life. The scriptures counsel us to:

1. Think Positively

    We are told to "gird up the loins of your mind" (I Peter 1:13), to "lift up [our] hearts and rejoice . . ." (D&C 27:15). We are even counseled on the focus of our thoughts with the direction to "Let thy bowels also be full of charity towards all men . . . let virtue garnish thy thoughts unceasingly" (D&C 121:45). We are also counseled by the Savior to "Look unto me in every thought; doubt not, fear not" (D&C 6:36).

    Paul gave counsel to think about "Whatsoever things are true, whatsoever things are honest, whatsoever things are just, whatsoever things are pure, whatsoever things are lovely, whatsoever things are of good report; if there be any praise think on these things" (Philippians 4:8).

    There should be no question as to the nature of our thoughts. We should think, feel and speak in a positive manner.

2. Attain a positive attitude

    Along with the counsel to think positively comes the counsel concerning the type of attitude that we should acquire. Perhaps the attitude is best described in the counsel given by the Savior himself when he indicated that our attitude should be one that reflects a conviction that "with God all things are possible" (Matthew 19:26).

3. Look to the future

    It is extremely easy to recall the negative experiences of the past that have been recorded in our brains. A review of these recordings often do not give us much hope for the future. Paul taught the Philippians to forget "those things which are behind, and [reach] forth unto those things which are before" (Philippians 3:13). Our outlook should be positive with a "renewing of [our] mind" (Romans 12:2). As we do this we will become more successful.

CONCLUSIONS

It is most important that we maintain a positive attitude if we expect to be successful either spiritually or temporally. Our thoughts, actions, and feelings are significant to success; therefore, we must be most aware of them and give the proper attention to our attitudes.

STEP III:
Learn

"He who adds not to his learning, diminishes it." — (The Talmud)

The steps to success are sequential, with the first step being to decide. After a decision is made, we must increase our belief in the Savior, in ourselves, and in others. With these two steps secured, we must develop a love for learning.

The process of becoming like God is to learn all things. That which we learn will be lasting. It has been revealed that "Whatever principle of intelligence we attain unto in this life, it will rise with us in the resurrection. And if a person gains more knowledge and intelligence in this life through his diligence and obedience than another, he will have so much the advantage in the world to come" (D&C 130:18-19).

The degree of our development is determined by the dimensions of our discoveries in this life. To live everlastingly is linked to our learning, for "It is impossible for a man to be saved in ignorance" (D&C 131:6). Our earthly experience is therefore limited only by our lack of a love for learning.

The Savior challenged "And ye shall know the truth, and the truth shall make you free" (John 8:32). The writer of Proverbs understood this principle well and concluded that "A wise man . . . will increase learning" (Proverbs 1:5).

President Spencer W. Kimball provided the proper perspective that learning should have in a person's life. "Spiritual training must take first place in our lives. Spiritual knowledge may be complimented with the secular in this life and for eternities, but the secular without the foundation of the spiritual is but like the foam upon milk, a fleeting shadow. Do not be deceived." (*Your Guide to the Institute Program of Religion,* p. 22.)

Satan will indeed attempt to deceive. He often deceives men of learning and uses them to disseminate his doctrine of deception. Many of the philosophies of our day are filled with half truths, and they attempt to deny that the source of all truth and success is found in the scriptures and in the counsel of the Brethren. They even deny the existence of Deity.

The *relativists* would have us believe that there are no absolute values or eternal laws, but that things are relative to the times and the society we live in; therefore, it's acceptable to "do your own thing." This is a philosophy of personal interpretation of right and wrong.

The *humanists* feel that the source of all success is in the individual, who must depend upon his own knowledge, skills, and strengths to achieve success. They depend upon their own reasoning to solve problems rather than personal revelations.

We have been warned concerning these men of learning who espouse these evil philosophies: "O that cunning plan of the evil one! O the vainness, and the frailties, and the foolishness of men! When they are learned they think they are wise, and they hearken not unto the counsel of God, for they set it aside, supposing they know of themselves, wherefore, their wisdom is foolishness and it profiteth them not. And they shall perish." (2 Nephi 9:28.) The counsel is concluded with the challenge that "to be learned is good if they hearken unto the counsels of God" (2 Nephi 9:29).

There are infinite things to be learned in this life; however, none seem to be more important than learning the process by which we perfect ourselves, and learning how to develop righteous relationships in the extended eternal family.

Preparation for Perfection 6

"By failing to prepare, you are preparing to fail."   —(Benjamin Franklin)

Our pursuit of perfection is a prime purpose for our presence in mortality. The Lord has placed much importance on the principle of preparation. He has counseled "Prepare ye, prepare ye for every needful thing" (D&C 88:119). He has also given a promise that "if ye are prepared ye shall not fear" (D&C 38:30).

If we are to be prepared, we must learn truth. We must not be deceived into thinking that we alone can discern and discover truth through our own methods. The scriptures tell us that it is "the Holy Ghost, that knoweth all things" (D&C 35:19), and that ". . . the spirit is truth" (1 John 5:6). It is by the power of the Holy Ghost that we may know the truth of all things and all things brought to our remembrance. (See John 14:26.)

Heavenly Father desires that each of His children gain knowledge. In the scriptures He has given us the process by which we can best obtain knowledge of earthly as well as eternal things. First, we must seek the Spirit, and under the direction and influence of the Spirit we should follow the process taught by the Savior to the Nephites as He instructed them to "go ye unto your homes [pause], and *ponder* upon the things which I have said, and ask [pray] of the Father, in my name, that ye may understand, and prepare your minds

[plan] for the morrow" (3 Nephi 17:3). The elements of this process are to pause, ponder, pray, and plan.

Pause

It takes time to prepare. There are many things that tend to take our time, but few have more importance than those things which will assist us in gaining perfection. We should determine a time and a place to prepare daily. Remember the Savior said, "go unto your homes." He emphasized the importance of a place where we can peacefully ponder these sacred things. As we pause, we must focus on using our time in a productive manner.

Ponder

To ponder is both to study and to meditate upon those things that have been memorized until they have been mastered.

1. Study

The scriptures suggest the special things that we should study. We are told to "search the scriptures" (John 5:39), to "seek ye out of the best books" (D&C 88:118), to "become acquainted with . . . languages" (D&C 90:15), and to "become acquainted with . . . people" (D&C 90:15).

This is an interesting process and one which the scriptures shed much light upon. The process of studying involves the actions of reading, seeking, and proving.

Read. Paul counseled Timothy to "give attendance to reading" (I Timothy 4:13). Without this initial step in studying, we are limited in what we can learn. We should work at increasing our reading rate and level of comprehension.

Seek. It is most important that we read with

our attention upon seeking facts, concepts, and principles. Random reading results in reduced retention. The Savior promised "seek and ye shall find" (Matthew 7:7). The Lord has given counsel that we should "seek words of wisdom" (D&C 88:118). Using this method, searching the scriptures will not seem to be work, but it will be a most worthwhile and enjoyable experience.

Prove. After reading and seeking truth, the next step is to "Prove all things; hold fast to that which is good" (I Thessalonians 5:21). We must internally process what we have found from our study of the scriptures. We should ask three questions in the proving process: Is it true? How does it fit with what I already know?, and does it replace what I once thought to be true?

2. Meditate

The process of meditation is more than a mental method; it is also a spiritual striving for the source of truth. The method of meditation is magnified as these steps are followed: Think, Feast, and Treasure.

Think. Paul instructed the saints to "think on these things" which they found to be true (Philippians 4:8). Thinking involves forming mental images in the mind and focusing intently.

Feast. Nephi counseled: "feast upon the words of Christ; for behold, the words of Christ will tell you all things what ye should do" (2 Nephi 32:3). To feast is to consume what we study, and what we study should be digested and absorbed into our being if it is to be lasting.

Treasure. After feasting upon the words, we should treasure them. The Lord said, "treasure up in your minds continually the words of life" (D&C 84:85). This implies that we should repeat those things learned in our minds and draw upon them in all our decisions.

Pray

Prayer is the process through which the veil is penetrated and allows us to communicate with Heavenly Father. This privilege is precious and should not be relegated to a low priority in our life. The scriptures teach us to pray continually (see Alma 13:28), and without ceasing (see I Thessalonians 5:17).

Heavenly Father has established a process for prayer that should be observed if we are to be effective in our communications with Him. The Savior taught the process to the Nephites when He said, "And whatsoever ye shall ask the Father in my name, which is right, believing that ye shall receive, behold it shall be given unto you" (3 Nephi 18:20). This process involves both our attitude and actions in order to receive answers.

1. Attitude

The proper attitude of prayer must be attained in order to communicate effectively. It involves preparing ourselves for this sacred experience of conversing with Deity.

The responses that we receive will be a reflection of our attitude. We should properly prepare ourselves for this experience by approaching the Lord with a sincere heart (see Moroni 10:4). Moroni counseled, "it is counted evil unto a man, if he shall pray and not with real intent of heart; yea, and it profiteth him nothing, for God receiveth none such" (Moroni 7:9). We must be honest with the

Lord with our intentions and expressions in full harmony.

We are also instructed to approach the Lord in a spirit of faith (see Moroni 10:4; 7:26; D&C 8:1; 18:18) and with a burning belief that we will receive what we have requested (see 3 Nephi 18:20, Moroni 7:26, D&C 8:1, 18:18). Without this proper attitude we cannot receive the answers that we anticipate.

2. Actions

There are basically five things that we may do in the process of praying. Each of these actions should be accomplished with a purpose in mind (see Moroni 10:4), and in the manner described by Moroni when he said, "Pray unto the Father with all the energy of heart" (Moroni 7:48).

Praise (Expressing). This is the part of the prayer where we express our gratitude to Heavenly Father and where we express our love for Him. This can be a most tender experience.

Petition (Asking). The Savior has counseled, "Ask and ye shall receive" (D&C 6:5). While "Father knoweth what things ye have need of, before ye ask him" (Matthew 6:8), He still expects us to ask for them. These petitions should be in the form of specific requests (see Moroni 7:26; 10:4; D&C 8:1; 46:7; 86:64). We must be careful that we not resort to "vain repetitions" (Matthew 6:7). While we should report to Father with regularity, our petitions should not be repetitious, ritualistic, or mere rote recitations.

Proposed (Presenting). The Savior said that we should "study it out in our [own] mind; and then [we must] ask [God] if it be right" (D&C 9:8). Our proposals should be carefully studied and well formulated before we present them for confirmation.

Profess (Confessing). We acknowledge before the Lord our weaknesses and our sins of omission and commission. We admit our faults and seek forgiveness for our transgressions. We should pour out our heart and bear our soul to the Lord as Enos did in "mighty prayer" (Enos 5:9). A spirit of contriteness should fill our heart as we labor long in this process of repentance.

Pause (Listening). A vital part of the prayer process is to pause and listen to the answers that we have sought. We must exercise patience and be receptive to the manifestations of the Spirit communicating comfort, counsel, and confirmation.

3. Answers

The Lord always answers prayers if they are properly presented. We must wait upon the Lord with patience and diligence for His answers. He has promised that we will receive that which we have petitioned for if it is expedient (see D&C 18:18; 88:64), if it is right for us (see 3 Nephi 18:20), and if we have petitioned with great faith (see Matthew 21:22).

He has also given us some guidance on the means by which He will manifest the answers to us.

METHOD	MANIFESTATION	SCRIPTURE
Impressions	•A peaceful feeling	D&C 6:23
	•A burning feeling in the bosom	D&C 9:8
	•A stupor of thought	D&C 9:9
	•An enlightenment of the mind with thoughts and impressions	D&C 6:15 D&C 8:2
Illumination	•Scriptures will illuminate with meanings magnified	Joseph Smith 2:12
Verbalization	•Still small voice	Enos 10
	•Spoken word	Moses 5:4
Visualization	•Visions	Alma 8:14-15
	•Dreams	1 Nephi 8:2
Visitations	•Angels	Alma 8:14-15
	•Holy Ghost	D&C 8:2-3
	•Father and the Savior	Joseph Smith 2:17

Plan

Planning is the final phase of the preparation process. We should not only prepare our minds but also plan for performance in the future. Thomas Huxley said, "The great end in life is not knowledge but action." Our knowledge of what we should do is not nearly as important as doing that which we know.

We must constantly be planning to apply principles in our lives by means of performance. After all, it is not those who proclaim the principles, but those who perform the principles who will be exalted.

Reaching Righteous Relationships 7

One of the great challenges in life is to cultivate celestial relationships in Heavenly Father's extended family. At times, our freedom to choose overcomes our capacity to control, and we create conditions that are contentious rather than compassionate.

Differences developed as the discussions between the Divine and the devilish began in the preexistence. With his discourse on decisions, Satan caused a division among the celestial family and was responsible for delivering one-third of the host of Heaven to their eternal destruction. He now continues this conflict and is continually promoting contention among Heavenly Father's children with the goal of total destruction, thus robbing them of their divine destiny.

Our ultimate celestial relationships are directly dependent upon the development of righteous relationships in this realm of existence. As we reflect upon these relationships, it becomes evident that we must become more aware of our responsibilities for others, our communications with others, and our responses to rejection from others. It is from these roots that we can reach righteous relationships.

RESPONSIBILITIES FOR OTHERS

Our eternal relationships are real. Failure to fully realize this is the reason for responses of resistance and rejection rather than reception and respect. It has been said "the Lord made us brothers because we need one another" (Bishop John H. Vanderberg, "My Brother's Keeper," *Ensign,* June 1971, p. 63).

The actions of many make it evident that they are asking the same question that Cain did in his state of anguish: "Am I my brother's keeper?" (Genesis 4:9). We are indeed our brother's keeper. The scriptures state that we have three major responsibilities in our relationships with our eternal relatives. We are to strengthen them, to share with them, and to serve them. This makes exaltation for everyone entirely possible.

Strengthen

The Savior challenged Peter ". . . when thou art converted, strengthen thy brethren" (Luke 22:32). We are also counseled to "succor the weak" (D&C 81:5). The counsel is even more specific in the ways that we should strengthen others: "Therefore, strengthen your brethren in all your conversations, in all your prayers, in all your exhortations and in all your doings" (D&C 108:7).

The following principles of relationships may be helpful to us as we accept this great responsibility that we have for others:

1. Accept them as they are.

    Paul instructed the saints to "receive ye one another, as Christ also received us . . ." (Romans 15:7). This counsel refers to *all* and it implies that we reject none. We often have difficulty discovering the difference in accepting and approving. We frequently use these terms to mean the same, and therefore we often avoid rather than accept certain people. The commandment is to accept all, but not to approve of all. The Savior loved the sinner, but not the sin. It is possible to accept a person and not to approve of his performance. This is our responsibility.

2. Make them feel important.

People are strengthened when they are made to feel important. We can instill this feeling in others when we take time to listen to them and discuss their interests. The Savior said let "Every man [seek] the interest of his neighbor . . ." (D&C 82:19).

3. Give positive feedback.

Every person needs to have honest but positive feedback concerning himself and his behavior. It is easy to become discouraged when we rarely receive positive responses from others. We are told that a "heaviness in the heart of man maketh it stoop; but a good word maketh it glad" (Proverbs 12:25). The Savior said to "lift the hands which hang down" (D&C 81:5). This will indeed strengthen any person.

4. Respect their feelings and opinions.

Respect shown to a person will increase his feeling of self-worth. The counsel is given to "let each esteem [respect] others better than themselves" (Philippians 2:3), and to "honour [respect] all men . . ." (1 Peter 2:17). The admonition that we should "condescend to men of low estate" (Romans 12:16) implies not only that respect is needed by everyone, but that this becomes one of our responsibilities to others.

5. Be their friend.

The Savior placed a high value on friendships, and He gave us some insights into the nature of this relationship. When we are friends, we will have affection and a deep regard for a person. The scriptures say that "a friend loveth at all times" (Proverbs 17:17). This is not a lightly regarded relationship. Friends understand each other and will lend support during days of difficulty (see D&C 121:9).

6. Trust others.

    Trust is sacred in a relationship, and it often leaves scars when it is severed. It is special because when we trust another person, we surrender a degree of our choice and control to them. It often involves a sharing of the soul's secrets. Trust is sometimes difficult to develop, and once it is shattered, it is often impossible to regain. Trust must always be earned, and it must endure if the relationship is to be a righteous one.

7. Treat them as you would like to be treated.

    This is the basis of a successful relationship. The Savior taught this principle when He said, "Therefore all things whatsoever ye would that men should do to you, do ye even so to them..." (Matthew 7:12).

8. Love them the most when they are the least lovable.

    Love is the most powerful principle on earth. It is the master of our motivations and the epitome of our emotions. Love is purest when given as the Savior gave it in a Christ-like form. The Lord said by way of commandment "... love thy neighbor as thyself" (Matthew 19:19), and "thou shalt live together in love..." (D&C 42:45). Love strengthens our relationships with others.

9. Take care of their needs.

    It is important to be aware of and give attention to the needs of others. As we become actively engaged in taking care of the needs of others, we will discover that others will often give careful attention to the care of our needs. Paul expressed this principle as he said, "Let everyone of us please his neighbor for his good to edification" (Romans 15:2).

10. Reconcile differences when they develop.

   This is a most important responsibility that we have for others, yet to some this becomes most difficult to do. The Savior said, "Go thy way unto thy brother, and first be reconciled to thy brother . . ." (3 Nephi 12:24; Matthew 5:24). This process of reconciliation involves two simple steps: We must *admit* any mistakes that we have made concerning the matter, then *ask* for forgiveness. It takes personal humility to humble others but through this process others can be reached. These humble actions will touch the spirit as they exhibit an absence of selfishness on our part, and therefore, decrease the possibility of defensiveness on the part of others.

11. Avoid passing quick judgements.

   The adversary is anxious to accelerate our assessments of others. We are often too quick to question the intelligence and integrity of others. Most quick judgements are made without the full facts for the formation of a fair judgement. The Savior cautioned "Judge not, that ye be not judged" (Matthew 7:1). There are two reasons that we often form faulty judgements. Sometimes we tend to look ". . . on the outward appearance. . ." (1 Samuel 16:7) rather than looking to the heart of a person. We may also be guilty of faulty perception and be as the one to whom it was said, "And why beholdest thou the mote that is in thy brother's eye, but perceiveth not the beam that is in thine own eye?" (Luke 6:41).

12. Avoid contention.

   Contention should be avoided because when

it prevails, peace perishes. The Savior and Satan use entirely opposite principles for resolving difficulties. The chart below summarizes these contrasting concepts:

SOURCE	PRINCIPLES	SCRIPTURES
SAVIOR	Counsel	Proverbs 11:14 Proverbs 15:20 Proverbs 20:18 Isaiah 8:10
	Communicate	1 Timothy 6:18 Hebrews 13:16
	Confront	Matthew 18:15-17 Luke 17:3 D&C 28:11 D&C 42:88, 92
SATAN	Criticize	John 6:43 1 Corinthians 10:10 Philippians 2:14
	Condemn	Luke 6:37
	Contend	D&C 10:63 3 Nephi 11:29

Share

The second responsibility that we have for others is to share that which we have with them. Paul taught that "none of us liveth to himself, and no man dieth to himself" (Romans 14:7). The scriptures state that we should share in the burdens of others and also share the gospel with them.

As we entered the waters of baptism, we took upon us a sacred covenant that we would be "willing to bear one another's burdens, that they may be light . . ." (Mosiah 18:8). Lending a helping hand is a holy responsibility that we have for others. During days of difficulty we also covenanted that we would be "willing to mourn with those that mourn, yea and comfort those that stand in need of comfort . . ." (Mosiah 18:9).

This sharing of compassion, this bearing of burdens not only makes life more bearable for others, but it also gives them the strength and feeling of security to become more successful.

We are also under covenant to Heavenly Father that we will "stand as witnesses of God at all times and in all things, and in all places . . . even until death. . ." (Mosiah 18:9). We have the sacred responsibility to share the gospel with those who are not yet members of the Church.

There are some who embrace the gospel, but who seem reluctant to share it with others. They are often selective as to whom they feel should receive these great truths. Father desires that *all* return to His presence and has set no constraints on their previous conditions, only on their present convictions. The Savior reminds us that He is "no respecter of persons, and will that all men shall know" (D&C 1:35; 38:16). He has spoken of several groups to whom the gospel should be shared:

GROUP	SCRIPTURES
Elect	D&C 29:7
Deceived	D&C 123:12
Despised	D&C 35:12-13
Poor	D&C 35:15
Lost	Matthew 8:11

In speaking to the shepherds, He said, "My sheep wandered through all the mountains, and upon every high hill: yea, my flock was scattered upon all the face of the earth, and none did search or seek after them" (Ezekiel 34:6). He challenged the elders to "search diligently and spare not" (D&C 84:94), and He gave them the promise "my sheep hear my voice and I know them, and they follow me" (John 10:27). Our responsibility is to seek after His sheep and share with them that which saves souls.

Serve

The Savior's life was one of service. He took time to care for the needs of others. He never expressed the thoughts "I'm too busy," "I'm too tired," "I don't have time," or "I don't care." These senseless sayings are only expressed by the slothful and not by the Savior. He knew well the eternal principle that "he that loseth his life for my sake shall find it" (Matthew 10:39; 16:25; Mark 8:35; Luke 9:24; 17:33). To lose one's life in service is to live eternally with the Savior.

Need we be reminded that "inasmuch as ye do it unto the least of these, ye do it unto me" (D&C 42:38; Matthew 25:40), or of the fact that "when ye are in the service of your fellow beings ye are only in the service of your God" (Mosiah 2:17)? As we understand this principle, we realize it is service that sanctifies the soul, and that it is the means through which we are saved.

COMMUNICATING WITH OTHERS

Communication is at the core of our relationship with others. It is important that we are aware not only of what we communicate but also the spirit in which we do so. Spirits can be softened or shattered, and feelings may overshadow the facts that have been said. The Savior warned that ". . . every idle word that men shall speak, they shall give account thereof in the day of judgement" (Matthew 12:36).

We have been given much counsel in the scriptures as to our communications with others. They can be classified by way of actions, articulations, and things to avoid.

COMMUNICATION	SCRIPTURES
•Speak softly	Colossians 4:6
•Look people in the eye	Proverbs 4:25
•Be direct and to the point	Matthew 5:37 3 Nephi 12:37
•Speak the truth	Ephesians 4:15 Proverbs 12:19 John 8:32
•Speak spiritual things	D&C 20:69
•Listen	James 2:19 Matthew 15:10 Proverbs 18:13 Proverbs 1:5 Proverbs 17:28

ACTIONS	SCRIPTURES
•Lying	Colossians 3:9 Proverbs 26:28 Matthew 19:18
•Gossiping	James 4:11
•Criticizing	John 6:43 1 Corinthians 10:10 Philippians 2:14
•Evil Speaking	James 4:11 Ephesians 4:29, 31 1 Corinthians 15:33
•Profanity & Vulgarity	Matthew 5:34 Colossians 3:8
•Complaining	D&C 9:6
•Foolish Questions	Titus 3:9
•Flattery	Proverbs 20:19 Job 17:5 Psalms 5:9 Psalms 12:2
•Anger	Proverbs 29:25 Proverbs 15:18 Matthew 5:22

Our communications reflect our countenance and our commitment. Righteous relationships are rooted in clean, caring, and convincing communications with others.

RESPONDING TO REJECTION

Rejection in any of its forms is extremely difficult to deal with. It dims our sense of self-worth. Heavenly Father realized that we would receive all forms of rejection even when we were involved in doing righteous things. He has given us much counsel in the scriptures on this subject by way of perspective and how to respond to rejection.

Perspective

If we fully understand the principle of rejection, we may gain strength as we realize that many times we will be rejected for righteousness' sake. The Savior said that we should not take it personally. He taught, "He that despiseth you despiseth me; and he that despiseth me despiseth him that sent me" (Luke 10:16; Thessalonians 4:8). It becomes clear that we may suffer as a part of the Savior's suffering. Peter clarified this concept as he spoke words of comfort saying, "But rejoice, inasmuch as ye are partakers of Christ's suffering..." (1 Peter 4:13).

We have the assurance that the Lord "healeth the broken heart, and bindeth up other wounds" (Proverbs 147:3). These sufferings and rejections will give us experience as they did the Prophet Joseph Smith as he was a prisoner in Liberty Jail. The Lord said, "Know thou, my son, that all things shall give thee experience and shall be for thy good" (D&C 122:7).

Responses

We can respond to rejection in any way we choose. Father desires that we not fall into the traps of the adversary as we exercise our freedom. He has given us wise counsel as to the ways we should respond to rejection in order to have a clear conscience.

RESPONSES	SCRIPTURES
Listen	James 1:19
Communicate	1 Timothy 6:18
Accept Criticism	1 Peter 2:20
Be in control of your answers	Proverbs 15:1 Proverbs 16:32 Proverbs 26:4 James 1:20 1 Peter 2:23
Get Counsel	D&C 121:9
Confront	Matthew 18:15-17 Luke 17:3 D&C 28:11 D&C 42:88, 92
Reprove	D&C 24:15 D&C 121:43 Mosiah 17:10
Turn the other cheek	Matthew 5:39-40
Do them a good deed	Matthew 5:44 Romans 12:2
Go the second mile	Matthew 5:40-41
Feed them	Romans 12:20
Pray for them	Matthew 12:20
Forgive them	Matthew 6:14-15 Matthew 18:21-22, 25-35 Luke 17:3 Luke 23:34
Bless them	Matthew 5:44 Romans 12:14
Love them	Matthew 5:44 Luke 6:27, 35-36

RESPONSES	SCRIPTURES
Do not worry	John 14:1
Do not respond in anger	D&C 19:30
Do not hold a grudge	Leviticus 19:18 Proverbs 24:29 James 5:9
Do not attempt to reason with an angry person	Proverbs 22:24-25 Alma 34:40-41
Do not fight back or do harm	Zechariah 8:17 Romans 12:17, 19
Do not contend	D&C 10:63 3 Nephi 11:29
Do not create strife	Philippians 2:3 II Thessalonians 2:24-25
Do not despise them	Matthew 18:10
Do not become bitter	Ephesians 4:31
Do not hate	Leviticus 19:17

A RIGHTEOUS EXAMPLE

Joseph, the favored son of Jacob, was greatly resented and ultimately rejected by his eleven brothers, who sold him to Ishmaelite merchants for twenty pieces of silver. He was taken into the land of Egypt and sold to Potiphar, who was the captain of the guard for Pharaoh.

Through all his trials and tribulations, Joseph remained a model of personal righteousness in his relationships with others. He exhibited many Christlike characteristics as he recognized his responsibilities for others, communicated his commitments, and responded in a righteous manner to the many rejections that he received.

Responsibility

One of Joseph's great characteristics was that of being a very responsible person. Shortly after his purchase by Potiphar, he "found grace in Potiphar's sight, and he served him..." (Genesis 39:4). As a result of his service to his new owner, and having the blessings of the Lord with him, Joseph was given a great responsibility, and Potiphar "made him overseer over his house, and all that he had he put into his hand" (Genesis 39:4).

Later when he was cast into prison, "the keeper of the prison committed to Joseph's hand all the prisoners that were in the prison; and whatsoever they did there, he was the doer of it" (Genesis 39:22). Joseph knew the power of the principle of service, and that even under conditions of prison or bondage, it would help him to prosper and be successful.

He felt a sense of responsibility to bear the burden of others and lift their spirits. It was Joseph who had the power and gift to interpret the dreams of Pharaoh's chief butler and his chief baker, and of Pharaoh himself.

Joseph never shirked his responsibility to share the gospel even at a time of extreme temptation. President Harold B. Lee said of Joseph, "He too, felt his great responsibility in bearing a true witness of the divine truths which he professed to believe" (Conference Report, April 1951, p. 34).

Communication

Joseph is a great example of one who maintained his control and communicated clearly under extreme pressure. It is interesting to see how he retained his righteousness as he communicated his convictions and commitments. Joseph went through the steps of refusing Potiphar's wife's advances, resisting her repeated requests, running as she removed his robe, and relying upon the Lord for his source of strength and protection.

When Potiphar's wife first approached Joseph, she "cast her eyes upon Joseph; and she said, Lie with me"

(Genesis 39:7). Joseph, without any reservation or hesitation, communicated his *refusal* in a most direct manner as the Savior had suggested "But let your communications be, yea, yea; nay, nay . . ." (Matthew 5:37). He also gave her the two reasons for his refusal of her request. He first expressed the great trust that her husband had in him and his desire to remain totally loyal to Potiphar. He also expressed his dismay at the thought of doing this "great wickedness, and [sinning] against God" (Genesis 39: 8, 9).

Potiphar's wife was persistent in her pleas for his pleasures and she "spake to Joseph day by day . . ." (Genesis 39:10). He continued to *resist* her request. It was said that he "hearkened not unto her, to lie by her, or to be with her" (Genesis 39:10).

The pressure finally became physical, and she "caught him by his garment, saying, Lie with me: and he left his garment in her hand, and fled, and got him out" (Genesis 39:12). As a result of his refusal, his resistance, and his running, he was thrown in prison on false charges.

Joseph relied heavily on the Lord for his protection under these preposterous circumstances. As a result of his righteousness "the Lord was with Joseph, and showed him mercy, and gave him favor in the sight of the keeper of the prison." (Genesis 39:21.) This was a great blessing of protection as under ordinary circumstances the charges of Potiphar's wife would have condemned Joseph to instant death.

Rejection

One of the more devastating forms of rejection is that given by relatives, by those who are our loved ones. Joseph received this form of rejection. He experienced the resentment of his relatives, and heard them plot to take his life as they expressed their hatred for him. He lost his freedom and was sold into bondage where he spent thirteen years of his life in slavery or in prison.

Even in the face of this rejection, he responded in a righteous manner. He did not become bitter; he did not blame his brothers or the Lord for the things that had beset him. Through all these degrading experiences he remained righteous, obedient to the commandments, and loyal to his owner.

It must have been a tender experience and a tremendous test of his testimony when he recognized his brothers when they came to Egypt to purchase food. It had been twenty-two years since he had seen them—twenty-two years since they had sold him in bondage and had stripped him of his birthright of freedom. He received his brothers and forgave them for their terrible transgression. He extended his love to them even though it was undeserved. He shared with them his substance without taking even a single shekel. This was truly a great example of one who knew well how to reach a righteous relationship with others.

STEP IV:
Act

"Knowing is not enough; we must apply. Willing is not enough, we must do."

— (Goethe)

Action is an extremely important step in the process of success. Without this step we have no promise for successful performance, yet many still seek success without this step. Henry Ford once said, "You can't build a reputation on what you are going to do." We cannot be successful on good intentions. Larry Eisenberg determined that "the smallest deed is better than the grandest intention."

The Lord has always counseled us to act. The scriptures are replete with admonitions to seek, search, watch, knock, gird up, awake, arise, go forth, proclaim, and to stand. With these action commandments comes the promise that "I the Lord am bound when ye *do* what I say, but when ye do not what I say, ye have no promise" (D&C 82:10).

This doctrine of doing is dependent upon our observation of the principle of obedience, the mastering of our motivation, and having a strong will to work. There can be no true success without applying the principles.

Observance of Obedience

8

Obedience is considered to be the first law of the Gospel. It is a principle of great importance. Samuel expressed that "to obey is better than sacrifice" (1 Samuel 15:22). It has also been said that obedience to the commandments is "the whole duty of men" (Ecclesiastes 12:13).

The Savior used this principle as the measure of our love for Him when He said, "If ye love me, keep my commandments" (John 14:15). Blessings are offered to each of us if we are obedient to the commandments. This law cannot be left nor taken lightly; it is stated simply that "There is a law, irrevocably decreed in heaven before the foundations of this world, upon which all blessings are predicated, and when we obtain any blessing from God, it is by obedience to that law upon which it is predicated" (D&C 130:20-21).

All success in life is directly dependent upon obedience to the principles that are involved. If we are to be successful in maintaining good health, we must be obedient to the laws of health. We cannot violate these laws and expect to be healthy.

Quality of Obedience

It is not enough to be obedient reluctantly. This violates the sacred intent of the law. We cannot be obedient by a mere acceptance of a principle and casually keep the commandment. We must do so with a real affection for the Savior and be motivated by this love rather than by the letter of the law.

The Savior said that we should "be *firm* in keeping the commandments . . ." (D&C 5:22), and "with all your might, mind and strength" (D&C 11:20). He also taught that He "requireth the heart and a willing mind . . ." (D&C 64:34). While these requirements were given for our spiritual development, they are also true for our temporal development. We must learn the principles and be obedient to them with firmness, intensity and willingness.

Examples of Obedience

There are many great examples of strong spirits who have been obedient. Their lives are a source of strength in our lives as we strive to be obedient.

Adam was an exceptional example of one who was most obedient. After being cast out of the Garden of Eden, he and Eve were desirous of discussing with the Lord the direction that they should take in their lives. They called upon the Lord, and He answered their petition and instructed them to offer up to Him a sacrifice of the firstlings of their flock. The scriptures say that "Adam was obedient unto the commandments of the Lord" (Moses 5:5). Later an angel was sent to them and tested the level of their obedience. He asked, "Why dost thou offer sacrifices unto the Lord?" (Moses 5:6). Adam answered the angel with purity and humility and said, "I know not, save the Lord commanded me" (Moses 5:6). Adam saw no need to justify or to doubt what he had done. He was completely obedient with an abiding faith in the Lord.

Noah was another strong spirit, a great example of one who was obedient. He served a lifelong mission preaching the gospel. Of all the great character traits that he possessed, perhaps none was stronger than his ability to obey. It was said of him "Thus did Noah; according to all that God commanded him, so did he" (Genesis 6:22).

Few have stood the trial of their faith and obeyed as did Abraham. The Lord made a tremendous request of Abraham when He said, "Take now thy son, thine only son Isaac, whom thou lovest, and get thee into the land of Moriah and offer him there for a burnt offering" (Genesis 22:2). Abraham never questioned the Lord, nor did he attempt to reason concerning this righteous request. He simply obeyed the Lord without reservation. As the knife was in position to slay his son, an angel of the Lord called Abraham and said, "Lay not thine hand upon the lad, neither do thou anything unto him" (Genesis 22:12). As a result of his great obedience, Abraham was blessed mightily by the Lord, who said, "I will bless thee, and in multiplying I will multiply thy seed as the stars of the heaven . . . and in thy seed shall all nations of the earth be blessed; *because thou hast obeyed my voice*" (Genesis 22:17-18).

The two thousand stripling sons of the people of Ammon were excellent examples of youth who were completely obedient to the things they had been taught by their mothers: "that if they did not doubt, God would deliver them" (Alma 56:47). Because of this belief, they became extremely courageous. Helaman, speaking of them to his brother Moroni, said, "never had I seen so great courage . . ." (Alma 56:45). It was said of them that "they were men who were true at all times in whatsoever thing they were entrusted" (Alma 53:20). They had this great faith and these character traits of courage, loyalty, and trust, because their mothers taught them "to keep the commandments of God and to walk uprightly before him" (Alma 53:21). As a result of their total obedience, they enjoyed the protection and blessings of the Lord, and none were slain in battle.

The most perfect example of obedience was that of the Savior. His entire life was one of loving obedience to His Father. He was always found doing His Father's will. Paul said of the Savior, "Though he were a Son, yet learned he obedience by the things which he suffered" (Hebrews 5:8).

There are times when obedience to a principle will test

our faith and may even cause us to suffer in order to reach success. Perhaps we should follow the counsel given by the Prophet Joseph Smith when he said, "I made this my rule: When the Lord commands, do it."

Mastering Motivation 9

"What every man needs most is something to get him to do what he can."
— (Ralph Waldo Emerson)

This temporal trip was designed for movement and mastery and not for mediocrity. These conditions are entirely within our control. Walter Russell expressed the fact that "mediocrity is self-inflicted and genius is self-bestowed."

It is sometimes easier to state our limitations than it is to extend our stride length and quicken the pace of our performance. If we truly understand the eternal evidences concerning our earthly experiences, we will accelerate our actions and achieve far beyond our present aspirations.

The Savior deeply desires that we master our motivation and not be consumed with laziness. His righteous indignation is clearly communicated in the counsel, "I would thou wert cold or hot. So then because thou art lukewarm, and neither cold or hot, I will spue thee out of my mouth" (Revelation 3:15-16).

MOTIVATIONAL MODEL

J. P. Morgan once said that "A man always has two good reasons for doing anything—a good reason and the real reason." Reasons regulate our responses. Our actions are not at all the results of accidents as we consciously or subconsciously choose our behaviors. There are several important concepts which should be considered.

1. We have the capacity to control our behavior through the choices we make.
2. Each choice carries with it one or more consequences ranging from pleasurable to painful.
3. The results of our actions are relayed to us in the form of feedback which stimulates, sustains, or stops our desire to continue the action.
4. Our divine destiny is deeply dependent upon these decisions and the driving forces which help us to determine them.

Motivation must be measured on an eternal level and not just by our earthly efforts. From the time of our spiritual birth, some were anxious to achieve, and their efforts were accelerated. The Lord showed Abraham the intelligences who were highly regarded and said, "Among all these there were many of the noble and great ones" (Abraham 3:22). These spirits were perhaps more highly motivated than the others. They not only accepted what had been taught, but they aspired to be obedient. They chose actions which enabled them to achieve much in that celestial condition. The Lord blessed them and said unto Abraham, "These I will make my rulers" (Abraham 3:23).

The veil did not void these advancements nor our aspirations to achieve. These recollections are reserved for a more righteous review after we pass through to the other side of the veil. It is important to understand the nature of our motivation:

1. The roots of personal motivation began with our spiritual birth.
2. Individuals differ in the degree and direction of their motivation; therefore, some are more easily motivated than others.
3. We are motivated both by internal and external influences.

4. It is possible to influence others and to be influenced by them.
5. There is a divine dimension that drives us to do good. "For it is God which worketh in you both to will and to do of his good pleasure" (Philippians 2:13). The Spirit is the greatest of all sources of motivation, yet there is no mention of this in motivational literature. The Spirit stimulates, stretches, and sustains us to succeed in a special way.

INTERNAL MOTIVATION

Socrates once said, "He who would move the world must first move himself." The Savior desires that we be self-starters and that our motivation be from within. He counseled, "For behold it is not meet that I should command in all things . . ." (D&C 58:26) but "men should . . . do many things of their own free will" (D&C 58:27). Internal motivation is based upon our aspirations, attitudes, arousal, and our abilities. When each of these are brought into action, our achievement will be accelerated.

Aspirations

An aspiration is an anticipation of achievement. Aspiration is based primarily upon our values, needs, and desires. From our values we identify our needs, which create our desires.

We usually aspire to those things which we value highly. The higher value that we place on a goal, the greater aspiration we will have to reach the goal.

Our basic needs are also a source of our aspirations. As an example, if we have a strong emotional need for attention, we will strongly aspire to those things which will gain attention. These needs can be physical, emotional, intellectual, social, or spiritual in nature.

From our values and needs we create strong desires. A desire is a craving or lust for something. Our desires become driving forces and powerful motivators.

Attitudes

There are many references in the scriptures as to the role attitude plays in motivation. The scriptures stress the importance of having an attitude of willingness, of hope, and of determination.

Paul taught that an attitude of willingness is important to proper performance when he said, "as there was a readiness to will, so there may be a performance also out of that which ye have" (2 Corinthians 8:11). He also was aware of the results that come when a person responds in a willing manner: "For if I do this thing willingly, I have a reward" (1 Corinthians 9:17).

As our faith increases, we will gain "a perfect brightness of hope . . ." (2 Nephi 31:20). Hope is seeing the light at the end of the tunnel and realizing the possibility of achievement. Without hope we will have only a limited amount of energy to expend toward our possible achievement.

The Savior was extremely determined in all that He did. There seemed to be an ever present determination which was an internal driving force. At the age of twelve when His parents found him in the temple, He responded to their concerns about His welfare saying, "Wist ye not that *I must* be about my Father's business?" (Luke 2:49). Later, as He was preaching in Capernaum, the people asked that He stay with them longer. He responded again with a determination in His voice, "I *must* preach the Kingdom of God in other cities also" (Luke 4:43). As His death grew near, He again expressed His determination saying, "I *must* work the works of him that sent me, while it is day: the night cometh when no man can work" (John 9:4).

Perhaps there is not recorded in the scriptures a stronger resolve of determination than that given by Paul to the Romans when he said, "For I am persuaded, that neither death, nor life, nor angels, nor principalities, nor powers, nor things present, nor things to come, nor height, nor depth, nor any other creature, shall be able to separate us from the love of God, which is in Christ Jesus our Lord" (Romans 8:38-39).

When we have a willing mind, a firm faith, a brightness of hope and a deep seated determination, we can truly do all things that we desire to do. These are the important aspects of our attitude to achieve.

Arousal

Dwight D. Eisenhower once said that "the great, driving forces of the world are not intellectual, but emotional." A self-motivated person will be excited about that which he is doing. As our emotions are aroused, we are stimulated to achieve. The mental excitement of enthusiasm creates a fervor, a passion to perform. An enthusiastic person burns within and has a glow that radiates to others.

Thinkers of every generation have pointed to the importance of enthusiasm in achievement. Disraeli said, "Every production of genius must be the production of enthusiasm." Emerson stated that "Enthusiasm is the mother of effort, and without it nothing great was ever accomplished."

There are several words in the scriptures used to describe enthusiasm. Paul spoke of being *"fervent* in spirit" (Romans 12:1), the Psalmists said, "My *zeal* has consumed me" (Psalms 119:129), and it was said of the Savior that "He is *beside* himself" (Mark 3:21).

We are admonished in the scriptures to be enthusiastic in all that we do. The counsel is given to "be *anxiously* engaged" (D&C 58:27), that we should attend to things "with great *earnestness*" (D&C 123:4), and it is "good to be *zealously* affected . . . ." (Galatians 4:18). The scriptures also say, "see that ye serve him with all your *heart, might, mind,* and *strength,* that ye may stand blameless before God at the last day." (D&C 4:2.)

Ability

We are motivated to do those things in which we are skilled to the degree that we receive satisfaction and enjoyment from them. We easily generate enthusiasm and energy when we are involved in activities in which we have abilities.

EXTERNAL MOTIVATION

There is an old adage which says, "You can lead a horse to water but you can't make him drink." This is an expression of truth; however, it should not be misunderstood. Our internal motivation can be significantly increased through the effort of others. Perhaps a more correct adage would say, "You can lead a horse to water, and get him to drink if you provide him with the salt that will create a thirst." The key to external motivation is finding the salt that is tantalizing to the taste.

The process of inspiring and influencing others is highly personal and must be designed to increase their levels of aspiration, attitude, arousal, and ability. This process involves a form of personal persuasion in an attempt to increase performance. Joseph Smith gave wise counsel concerning the spirit in which this should be done when he said, "No power or influence can or ought to be maintained by virtue of the priesthood, only by persuasion, by longsuffering [patience], by gentleness and meekness [kindness], and by love unfeigned" (D&C 121:41). Through this kind, loving, and patient persuasion hearts can be softened, souls can be strengthened and success can be secured.

There are four basic techniques which are most important in the process of motivating others to greater performance and achievement. These techniques are modeling, communicating, rewarding, and challenging. Contained in these techniques is the salt to stimulate and stir the spirits of others.

Modeling

One of the most powerful motivational techniques is that of modeling the behavior that you desire to see in others. Great leaders are always great models and examples of excellence in performance. The Savior said, "follow me. . ." (Matthew 4:19), and He counseled us to be "even as I" (3 Nephi 27:27).

There is a need for people whom we can look up to, who set a proper example for us, and even be our heroes. From them, we gain great strength and confidence as we make choices in our lives.

Communicating

It is very important to use the power of communication to inspire others. When a desirable behavior is verbally reinforced, it tends to be sustained and even strengthened. This simple technique fulfills many needs in those who receive it. Isaiah counseled, "Say ye to the righteous, that it shall be well with them. . ." (2 Nephi 13:10). He realized both the reasons for and the results of reinforcing righteous behavior.

Heavenly Father gave verbal support to the Savior on the occasions when He was introduced to others. Father said, "This is my beloved Son in whom I am well pleased" (Matthew 17:5; see also 3 Nephi 11:7; and Joseph Smith 2:17).

This verbal support is given to others in the form of communicating assurance, approval, appreciation, encouragement, praise, recognition, respect, and strength.

1. Assurance
People seek assurances that they are doing well and that they are taking the right course of action. A feeling of assurance dispels feelings of uncertainty and insecurity. Paul recognized this important need and related that the Lord "hath given assurance unto all men. . ." (Acts 19:31).

2. Approval

When we receive approval from those who are important in our lives, we are motivated to continue what has been approved. Paul taught this technique in his counsel "That ye may approve things that are excellent; that ye may be sincere..." (Philippians 1:10). He gave the two keys in communicating approval to others: the behavior should be worthy of approval, and you must be sincere in your communications. He understood that false flattery is fatal in our relationships with others.

In the parable of the talents, the Lord gave approval to those who had the two and five talents and who had magnified their talents. He said to them, "Well done thou good and faithful servant; thou has been faithful over a few things, I will make thee ruler over many things..." (Matthew 25:21-23). He rebuked the one who had hid his only talent. He said, "Thou wicked and slothful servant ..." (Matthew 25:26). There is an important principle in this parable concerning approval. The Lord gave equal approval to the two who had done well even though what they had done was not equal. Approval should be based upon personal accomplishments and not on comparative accomplishments.

3. Appreciation

The showing of appreciation lifts the spirits and feelings of self-worth in others. These elevated feelings motivate people to higher levels. It is most important to express appreciation for a job well done. Paul, in speaking to the Thessalonians, said, "In everything give thanks . . ." (1 Thessalonians 5:18).

4. Encouragement

Encouragement gives life to the lowly and lifts

the load of the heavy hearted. We are counseled, "For if they fall, the one will lift up his fellow" (Ecclesiastes 4:10). Paul admonished, "Wherefore lift up [encourage] the hands which hang down, and the feeble knees" (Hebrews 12:12). Kind and encouraging words do lift spirits, lighten loads and give new life to those who are low.

5. Enthusiasm

That burning within which glows and radiates can reach others and kindle a desire to accelerate their pace. Paul recognized the contagious nature of enthusiasm as he reminded the Corinthians, ". . . your zeal [enthusiasm] hath provoked [inspired] very many" (2 Corinthians 9:2).

6. Praise

Paul taught the saints in Rome that a natural response to righteous actions is praise. He said, "do that which is good, and thou shalt have praise of the same" (Romans 13:3). Praise can be an effective technique even when a person's efforts have not resulted in excellence. Franklin Jones said that "praise is a device for making a man deserve it."

7. Recognition

Acknowledging a person focuses attention on their activities or accomplishments. It is an act of courtesy which shows concern and consideration for them. It offers them a sense of status and personal security. As we recognize others, they will respond toward increased results.

8. Respect

A communication of respect is a form of bestowing an honor on people. It indicates that we regard them highly. Showing respect causes people to respond with an increased sense of dignity and dedication. It is most important to respect their

9. **Strengths**
    We should communicate strengths to those we hope to motivate. While it is appropriate to deal with weaknesses, these should not dominate our discussions. The Savior challenged Peter, "strengthen thy brethren" (Luke 22:32). The Lord has given us the specific ways that we can strengthen others and therefore help them to become more motivated. He said to communicate strength "in all your *conversations,* in all your *prayers,* in all your *exhortations,* and in all your *doings*" (D&C 108:7).

Rewarding

The Lord has always rewarded His children according to the works that they have performed. This principle is a permanent part of motivating righteous behavior. He has reasoned that "if ye sow good ye shall also reap good for your reward" (D&C 6:33). The principle is plainly given that "every man shall receive his own reward according to his own labor" (1 Corinthians 3:8).

This principle is applied frequently throughout the scriptures. The Lord often gives the principle with a promise and a punishment. This places His children in a position to choose with no reservations as to what His response will be.

The same concept should be applied in motivating others. Results should be rewarded; however, care should be taken that all positive behavior and achievements do not need rewarding in an immediate or visible manner. This is consistent with the manner in which the Lord rewards the righteous; we receive many blessings from Him that go unnoticed, but they are still given.

Challenging

People are motivated when they are called upon to meet a challenge, to make a conquest or to meet a commitment. Their motivation is increased when this challenge is clearly communicated in the form of expectations, goals, or responsibilities set. Motivation is further increased when these challenges are followed with a request for a commitment. When people know what is expected of them, they develop a desire to live up to those expectations. When we share our expectations with them, we are showing them the level at which we expect them to perform. This in turn gives them a sense of security as they strive to meet these expectations. The Lord has always expected much from His children, and if we are to inspire and to influence others, we too must expect levels of excellence from them.

People are motivated by challenging goals. While it is important for people to set their own personal, professional, and gospel-related goals, they are stimulated when organizational goals are set from which they can establish their own. Frank Goble, a management consultant, placed great emphasis on goal setting as a motivator when he said, "The establishment of challenging, measurable goals is probably one of the most powerful motivating techniques of modern management" (*Excellence in Leadership,* American Management Association, 1972, p. 103).

When people are given responsibility, with the freedom to function, they become excited. President David O. McKay pointed to the importance of this challenge when he said, "Man's responsibility is correspondingly operative with his free agency."

CONTRASTING EXAMPLES

Throughout this chapter, various internal and external motivational techniques have been scripturally supported as they have been proven to be successful. There are, however, in the scriptures two contrasting styles of motivation which have been used from the beginning in the great conflict between the Savior and Satan. These styles have their own characteristics, methods, and ultimate results. We should clearly understand the differences in these two styles, for there is no middle ground.

Jacob taught the need for "opposition in all things" (2 Nephi 2:11). The management and motivational styles of the Savior and Satan reflect this righteous principle. The Savior's style was characterized as a way of light rather than darkness. It was He, who said, "I am the light of the world; he that followeth me shall not walk in darkness but shall have the light of life" (John 8:12). He motivates people through enlightenment, teaching them the truth. Satan, of course, chose to keep people in a state of darkness as "The way of the wicked is darkness" (Proverbs 4:19). Each of their methods are based upon these contrasting characteristics.

It was the contrast between choice and control which was at the core of the conflict in the celestial councils. The methods of the Savior pertain to freedom rather than force; therefore, it is understandable that the Savior motivates by persuasion rather than by pressure (see D&C 121:39), and encourages us by way of faith and not by means of fear.

The Savior works from a base of fixed principles, while Satan struggles with flexible philosophies. The teachings of the Savior are to love one another instead of having lust for each other. He teaches that it is the principle of preparation which leads to perfection rather than the principle of procrastination, which is professed by Satan. We are motivated by the Savior to become selfless rather than selfish as Satan would have us be, and to serve instead of being served.

It should be no surprise that the Savior has given us the power of discernment that we may "discern between the righteous and the wicked . . ." (D&C 101:95), while Satan uses the power of deception to "blind men, and to lead them captive at his will. . ." (Moses 4:4).

The Savior desires that we be dedicated while Satan

demands that we be defiant and disobedient. We can be motivated to become saints and live with the Savior, or we can choose to live as one of Satan's slaves.

SUMMARY

Mastering motivation is significant to our success. We become highly motivated when we realize our internal motivator, respond to our external motivator, and receive and are touched by the Spirit.

The source of our internal motivation is clearly related to the intensity of our aspirations, attitudes, arousal, and ability. To increase our energy and our efforts, we must be personally in control of these aspects of our living.

If we are to be stimulated and stretched by others, they too must be aware of these internal sources of motivation. All that they do by means of experiences or encouragements must touch these factors.

When we are touched by the Spirit, our souls will be instantly stretched, and we will feel sustaining and strengthening influences in our lives. This is a pure and perfect motivational process.

Will to Work 10

As a result of our obedience to the commandments and the mastery of our motivation, we should have an increased desire to work, to toil with the talents we have been given, to exert energy in our pursuit of excellence, and to perform until we have reached a state of perfection. The Lord has spoken on the principles of work, and of laziness, and He has given us great examples to follow.

WORK

We are placed on this earth to work...
— (President David O. McKay)

The scriptures tell us that work is essential, and that it is a commandment. They point to desirable work habits and to the ultimate value of work itself.

This doctrine of doing is *essential* to our exaltation. Elder David O. McKay reminded us that "There is no salvation without work . . ." (Conference Report, October 1909, p. 90.) The Savior Himself taught this doctrine as He said that "he shall reward every man according to his works" (Matthew 16:27). A denial of the importance of our deeds will lead to our ultimate destruction. Toil is still the only means by which we can increase our talents. Success in this life is dependent upon our diligence and actions rather than upon our dreams of doing. President Spencer W. Kimball said, "Success is reserved for those who work at it, those not afraid of the midnight oil." (*The Teachings of Spencer W. Kimball* [Bookcraft: Salt Lake City], p. 360.) He taught this principle by way of the marvelous example that he set in stretching himself and laboring for long hours. Whatever we want, we must be willing to work for it. If we want to win, to gain wealth, or become wise, we must pay the price in order to gain these things. There are no shortcuts to success; its pathway is still straight, and it is best traveled by means of an expenditure of energy.

The Lord has given us the *commandment* to work, to earn our living by the sweat of our brow, as He counsels, "Six days thou shalt do thy work, and on the seventh day thou shalt rest . . ." (Exodus 23:12.) He clearly intends that we continue to work and make wise use of the time that He has given for us.

He has not only given us the commandment to work, but He has also instructed us to form healthy work habits. Paul counseled, "whatsoever ye do, do it heartily . . ." (Colossians 3:23). This was the same admonition given by the Lord as He said, "labor with your might" (D&C 75:3). While we are counseled by the Savior to go the second mile, doing more than is required (see Matthew 5:41), He also cautions that we should "not run faster or labor more than [we] have strength and means provided . . ." (D&C 10:4). This pacing of our performance gives us not only a protection but also an increased productivity. If we follow this counsel, we will find great enjoyment in our work, for the scriptures say, "there is nothing better, than a man should rejoice in his own work. . ." (Ecclesiastes 4:22).

There are many *values* that we will receive if we are willing to work. Our bodies are designed for doing; therefore, the Lord has provided a way to health through work. We will be able to rest and to relax better for "The sleep of a laboring man is sweet . . ." (Ecclesiastes 5:12). Alma said, "the Lord doth give me exceeding great joy in the fruit of my labors" (Alma 36:25); therefore, we will gain great satisfaction in our accomplishments. We can also receive temporal blessings if we are willing to work for them, and if we do so in wisdom, as we are promised, "In all labor there is profit" (Proverbs 14:23).

LAZINESS

> There is no curse equal to the curse of idleness...
> —(J. Reuben Clark, Jr.)

The Lord has given us much insight in His lessons on laziness. We should realize from these recitations that we have received commandments on this matter, that we should recognize the characteristics of idleness, and that we should be aware of His warnings that have been given.

The Lord has much indignation for those who choose to be idle, and He has given the *commandment* "Thou shalt not idle away thy time..." (D&C 60:13). This commandment is clear, and we should recognize the righteous reason for this request for this is the time we must use "to prepare to meet God..." (Alma 12:24).

It is not difficult to recognize the *characteristics* of those who are lazy. They are not interested in overcoming their inertia. They are quietly content in their state of complacency. They resist any responsibilities which may interfere with their rest. Those who do accept assignments soon become apathetic and slothful in their service. This stagnation is a strategy of Satan and produces failure rather than success. There are still other characteristics mentioned in the scriptures. The lazy love sleep (see Proverbs 6:9), they are wasteful (see Proverbs 18:9), and are often greedy (see D&C 56:17).

We have been given the *warning* "He that is slothful shall not be counted worthy to stand..." (D&C 107:100). The judgements of the Lord stand against those who are lazy in this life. The Lord counts them as being "worse than an infidel" (1 Timothy 5:8). He has decreed that "the idler shall not have place in the Church, except he repent and mend his ways" (D&C 75:29), and that they "shall not eat the bread nor wear the garments of the laborer" (D&C 42:42, see also 2 Thessalonians 3:10).

EXAMPLES

Few stories in the scriptures are more beautiful than the fourteen-year labor for love by Jacob for his beautiful wife, Rachel. From the time that he first saw her at the well, he loved her and was willing to work for her hand in marriage. He said to her father Laban, "I will serve thee seven years for Rachel thy younger daughter" (Genesis 29:18). He lived up to his commitment and "served seven years for Rachel; and they seemed unto him but a few days, for the love he had to her" (Genesis 29:20). After successfully serving Laban for the seven years, "Jacob said unto Laban, give me my wife, for my days are fulfilled that I may go in unto her" (Genesis 29:21). Laban brought his older and less desirable daughter Leah to marry Jacob, thus deceiving him. When Jacob challenged Laban on this matter of matrimony, he was told that he would be given Rachel for his second wife, but he must labor another seven years after he received her. Rachel then bore Jacob his beloved son Joseph.
beloved Rachel, who later bore him his son Joseph.

Moses was one of the greatest spirits who ever lived on earth. He was often used as a standard of comparison, and as a model for others to follow. The Lord said of him "thou art in the similitude of mine Only Begotten . . ." (Moses 1:6). Moses had a strong will to work. He labored for forty years leading the children of Israel out of Egyptian bondage. He had the foresight and tenacity to finish a task. He was willing to do all that was necessary to accomplish that which was assigned.

Jacob and Moses should serve as great models to each of us as we increase our willingness to work. We should do so with a great strength of will and energy. If we do as they have done, we will be successful.

STEP V:
Endure

"Behold we count them happy which endure.
— (James 5:11)

We have now approached the fifth and final step to success. It is during this step that we are called upon to bear burdens, to withstand weariness, to prove our potential, and to stand steadfastly. As a result of these experiences, our souls will be stretched, our spirits will be strengthened, our character will be created, our testimonies tested, and our success will be secured.

Many, however, stumble and stray by the wayside, too weary to walk. The sanctification process is too much of a struggle. They see no advantages in their adversities, and are no longer able to bear their burdens or to overcome their obstacles. They fail to fight to the finish or to endure to the end.

The Lord has provided the principles whereby all may safely pass through their tribulations and endure their personal Garden of Gethsemane, thus growing into Godhood. To do this we must have answers about adversity, understand the power of personal perseverance, and accept a challenge for completion.

Answers About Adversity 11

"He that wrestles with us strengthens our nerves and sharpens our skill. Our antagonist is our helper."

— (Edmund Burke)

Adversity comes in the form of afflictions, trials, tribulations, and trouble. It is part of that eternal experience of testing, trying, and proving through which each of us must pass. It may even cause pain, suffering, and sorrow, but we have the assurance that "no pain suffered by man or woman upon the earth will be without its compensating effects if it be suffered in resignation and if it be met with patience" (President Spencer W. Kimball, *The Teachings of Spencer W. Kimball* [Salt Lake City: Bookcraft], p. 168).

We should recognize that there are some advantages in the adversity that we may face. Adversity amplifies our attitudes, attributes, and actions. Adversity helps us to appear as we actually are. As we experience adversity, we gain a greater self-awareness and are able to accurately assess our strengths and weaknesses. We can then make the appropriate adjustments of those things we must accept and those we must alter if we are to reach the celestial kingdom.

People respond to adversity with different attitudes and actions. Some are bewildered and feel beaten by the burdens that they are called to bear. Some place blame on others and even border on blasphemy. The true believer will see the blessings that can be gained. It is true that "adversity causes some men to break; others to break records" (William Arthur Ward). Elder Neal A. Maxwell explained it best when he expressed, "The winds of tribulation, which blow out some men's candle of commitment, only fan the fires of faith of others" (Conference Report, October 1975, p. 15).

NONE ARE EXEMPT

Adversity will be a part of every person's life in mortality. There are no exceptions to this eternal principle. Without adversity, no soul can be sanctified to the degree that it could become divine in nature and abide in the presence of Heavenly Father.

The *Savior* Himself suffered the severities of this life. Alma prophesied of the Savior saying He would "go forth, suffering pains and afflictions and temptations of every kind. . ." (Alma 7:11). President Spencer W. Kimball said, "The sufferings of the Savior were part of His education." This was the most comprehensive education ever given in mortality. He "descended below all things, in that he comprehended all things, that he might be in all and through all things, the light of truth" (D&C 88:6). He not only knows all, but He has suffered all, and has overcome all that we might have the possibility of perfection. It was said that through it all He learned "obedience by the things which he suffered" (Hebrews 5:8). After all of this, He said, "be of good cheer; I have overcome the world" (John 16:33).

The *prophets* have no promise that they will be preserved without the presence of adversity. To be so promised would be in contrast to the celestial counsel given by the Savior when He said, "Take, my brethren, the prophets, who have spoken in the name of the Lord, for an example of suffering affliction, and of patience:" (James 5:10). Their examples of excellence are for us to follow.

Job is an example of a righteous man who suffered and overcame many afflictions in his life. He was a most righteous person; in fact, the Lord said of Job, "there is none like him in the earth, a perfect and an upright man. . ." (Job 1:8). Not only was Job extremely righteous, but he was also very wealthy. Satan desired to destroy Job and challenged the Lord to "put forth thine hand now, and touch all that he [Job] hath, and he will curse thee to thy face" (Job 1:11). The arrogance of the adversary was very evident in his words. The Lord had great faith in Job and decided to test him in the face of adversity. Job was offered to Satan with the restriction that his life could not be taken. He suffered great adversity; his servants were slain, his animals were stolen and later slain, his sheep were burned, and even his children were killed. Job responded to these great adversities with the attitude ". . . the Lord gave, and the Lord hath taken away; blessed be the name of the Lord" (Job 1:21). His testimony was tried, but he remained true. His afflictions were not over, more adversity was added. He then experienced boils that covered his body causing much pain, and while in this state of physical suffering, he was tempted by his wife to "curse God, and die. . ." (Job 2:9). It was said that "his grief was very great" (Job 2:13). He acknowledged that "Fear came upon me, and trembling, which made all my bones to shake" (Job 4:14). Job later described his condition in his own words expressing the anguish and agony that he was experiencing.

> He hath stripped me of my glory, and taken the crown from my head. He hath destroyed me on every side, and I am gone: and mine hope hath he removed like a tree. He hath also kindled his wrath against me, and he counteth me unto him as one of his enemies. His troops come together, and raise up their way against me, and encamp round about my tabernacle. He hath put my brethren far from me, and mine acquaintance are verily estranged from me. My kinsfolk have failed, and my familiar friends have forgotten me. They that dwell in mine house, and my maids, count me for a stranger: I am an alien in their sight. I called my servant, and he gave me no answer; I intreated him with my mouth.

> My breath is strange to my wife, though I intreated for the children's sake of mine own body. Yea, young children despised me; I arose, and they spake against me. All my inward friends abhorred me: and they whom I loved are turned against me. My bone cleaveth to my skin and to my flesh, and I am escaped with the skin of my teeth. (Job 19:9-20.)

Job was stripped of his substance, his strength, and his support system. There was nothing left but the strength of his spirit. He bore a touching testimony when he said, "For I know that my redeemer liveth, and that he shall stand at the latter day upon the earth: and though after my skin worms destroy this body, yet in my flesh shall I see God" (Job 19:25-26).

Paul, the Apostle, suffered much in his ministry. He expressed his condition to the Corinthian saints saying, "For out of much affliction and anguish of heart I wrote unto you with many tears" (2 Corinthians 2:4). His attitude remained positive in the face of adversity. He wrote "We are troubled on every side, yet not distressed; we are perplexed, but not in despair; persecuted, but not forsaken; cast down, but not destroyed" (2 Corinthians 4:8-9). In a later epistle he expressed, "Therefore I take pleasure in infirmities, in reproaches, in necessities, in persecutions, in distresses for Christ's sake . . . then am I strong" (2 Corinthians 12:10). Strength can be gained through suffering.

The prophet Joseph Smith endured much during his earthly experience. He was born into poverty, suffered illnesses and indignities, was falsely accused and cursed for his communications with Deity. He was driven from his family and his followers; harassed and hunted for his humble testimony of truth. He was insulted and illegally imprisoned, yet he defended his faith. He was painfully persecuted, tortured and taunted, but he would not deny his testimony. He was willing with his Christlike conduct and his commitment to the cause to let his life be taken at the age of 38. Joseph stood the test of his time, and it was said of him,

"Joseph Smith, the Prophet and Seer of the Lord, has done more, save Jesus only, for the salvation of men in this world, than any other man that ever lived in it" (D&C 135:3).

President Spencer W. Kimball was no stranger to struggle in this life. This choice spirit of our Heavenly Father also experienced the refining process that comes to the righteous. As a result he was greatly strengthened. His life was spared from death by drowning, and from disease while still in his youth. At a tender age he survived facial paralysis and the loss of his mother. As a General Authority he lived through several heart attacks, open heart surgery, cancer of the throat, Bell's palsy, and an automobile accident. Through it all, he lengthened his stride and quickened his pace.

SOURCES OF ADVERSITY

Answers concerning our personal adversity are not always clear; however, the scriptures give us some suggestions as to the source of these adversities. The indication is that there are three sources from which we may experience our sufferings. It may be self-imposed, Satan-imposed, or Savior-imposed.

Self-Imposed Adversity

There is no doubt that we impose certain adversity upon ourselves. This happens as the result of the choices we make. Difficulty often develops through three types of decisions that are made. There are times when we make careless choices. We give some thought to these choices, but we do not give them our careful consideration. The consequences of this type of choice may not cause much anguish or suffering, but when such a pattern develops, we may experience difficulty. The second type is a carefree choice. We give little or no thought to the possible consequences even though we have no evil intents when we make the choice. The consequences could be more condemning than those of a careless choice. The third type choice is a calculated choice in which we make a deliberate decision to be disobedient. These consequences can be such that we suffer physically, emotionally, and spiritually even to the point where we are separated from the Spirit.

Satan-Imposed Adversity

Satan is dedicated to the destruction of our souls, and in the process, he will deal us as much suffering and misery as possible. The Lord summarized the mission of Satan when He said, "Satan seeketh to destroy. . ." (D&C 132:77). Satan's personal battle with each of us is but a small part of his battle from the beginning with the Savior. It has been taught that "Satan . . . knew not the mind of God, wherefore he sought to destroy the world" (Moses 4:6). He is indeed the "enemy unto God, and fighteth against him continually. . ." (Moroni 7:12). The battle for the destruction of our eternal destiny is a constant one. Satan has his armies ready to launch agonizing attacks on all of Heavenly Father's children. We should recognize the types of weapons that he uses to win his wars. They come in the form of temptations, contentions, lies, and deceptions.

When we are confronted with *temptations,* we can be assured that this form of adversity is from Satan who "enticeth [us] to sin and to do that which is evil continually" (Moroni 7:12). At times these temptations are difficult and demand divine powers to provide us protection. Satan can be commanded to depart from our presence, giving some relief from these pressures.

Another weapon of Satan is that of *contention* for he "doth stir up the hearts of the people to contention. . ." (D&C 10:63). He is the "father of all lies. . ." (Moses 4:4), and he uses this device to *"deceive* and to blind men. . ." (Moses 4:4). There are powerful personal ploys that are used to make our lives more difficult. Satan continuously "maketh war with the saints of God. . ." (D&C 76:29).

Satan often applies his greatest adversity at a time prior to or immediately following our most special spiritual experiences or at a time when we receive sacred assignments. This has been his pattern from the beginning. He attempted to destroy Moses immediately after Moses had seen God and had been permitted to see sacred things. (See Moses 1:12-20.) Satan appeared to Moses and attempted to get Moses to worship him. He lied to Moses and "cried with a loud voice and rent upon the earth, and commanded, saying: I am the Only Begotten, worship me" (Moses 1:19). The experience was intense. ". . . Moses began to fear exceedingly; and as he began to fear, he saw the bitterness of hell. . ." (Moses 1:20). But though he was sorely tempted, like our Savior, he prevailed in righteousness and was blessed with even greater things.

Savior-Imposed Adversity

The Savior has a great love for each of us and makes divine judgements that sometimes involve the use of adversity. The scriptures indicate that His use of adversity may be for two righteous reasons, either for corrective purposes or for creative purposes.

The Lord has always indicated that He loves us enough to correct us. This loving correction serves the purposes of calling us to repentance, helping us to remember Him, giving us promised punishments, and teaching us the things that we need to learn.

The Lord told Joseph Smith, "whom I love I also chasten that their sins may be forgiven. . ." (D&C 95:1). Again He instructed the Prophet when He said, "And inasmuch as they sinned they might be chastened, that they might repent" (D&C 1:27). His corrections cause us to remember Him. This principle may be puzzling to some, but it is true to our nature. The Lord spoke to the nature of man when he explained, "In the day of their peace they esteemed lightly my counsel; but, in the day of their trouble, of necessity they feel after me" (D&C 101:8). Helaman said, "except the Lord doth chasten his people with many afflictions, yea, except he doth visit them with death and with terror, and with famine and with all manner of pestilence, they will not remember him" (Helaman 12:3). Some adversity is given by the Lord to apply punishment to His children as He said, "I, the Lord, have suffered the affliction to come upon them, wherewith they have been afflicted, in consequence of their transgressions" (D&C 101:2). Suffering sometimes serves as a *schooling* in order to strengthen us. The Lord said, "And my people must needs be chastened until they learn obedience, if it must needs be, by the things which they suffer" (D&C 105:6).

The *creative* purposes of adversity are shown in the scriptures. There are several sacred purposes for which the Lord uses adversity. The things which we suffer give us experience, test us, strengthen us, and serve as a means through which we can be blessed. He told the prophet Joseph Smith that "all these things shall give thee experience, and shall be for thy good" (D&C 122:7). It is through the use of adversity that we are tested and proven in all things. One of the great purposes for coming to earth is to be "tried in all things that [we] may be prepared to receive the glory" (D&C that has been prepared for us (D&C 136:31). When we perform under pressure, we increase the possibility of being strengthened. We gain strength only by stretching our capabilities; and without this increased demand our development will be limited. The Lord also uses adversity as a means of bestowing *blessings* upon His children. There is the great principle that "after much tribulation come the blessings. . ." (D&C 58:4).

COUNSEL OF COMFORT

"In the world ye shall have tribulation: but be of good cheer; I have overcome the world."

—(John 16:33)

During our darkest hours we often experience feelings of disappointment, discouragement, and even depression. The agony we feel may seem to be more than we can bear. We should remember that the Savior, in the process of overcoming all things, experienced the greatest suffering of all. His suffering was so great that only He could properly describe it. He said that it "caused myself, even God, the greatest of all, to tremble because of pain, and to bleed at every pore, and to suffer both body and spirit. . ." (D&C 19:18). The Savior is the perfect model for each of us to follow as we experience suffering and anguish of heart. He has given us great counsel that will be helpful in overcoming these things in our lives. His counsel will help improve our attitudes toward our adversities.

Our *attitudes* are important in dealing with our difficulties. As we are tried and tested we should increase our trust in the Lord. Alma counseled his son Shiblon, "put your trust in God even so much ye shall be delivered out of your trials, and your troubles and your afflictions. . ." (Alma 38:5). We are counseled to "Trust in the Lord with all thine heart; and lean not unto thine own understanding" (Proverbs 3:5). As we increase our trust in the Lord, we will reduce the intensity of our worry.

The Savior said, "Let not your heart be troubled, neither let it be afraid" (John 14:27). As we experience the pains of life, we are counseled to be patient. This allows us to act in a responsible manner instead of reacting in a less desirable or destructive way. We often expect instant solutions to serious situations; however, instant relief rarely refines us or helps us to become more righteous. The Lord counsels, "Be patient in afflictions, for thou shalt have many; but endure them. . ." (D&C 24:8).

There are three basic *actions* that we are counseled to take when we face adversity. We should pray, study the scriptures, and seek the Spirit. These actions will give us the strength needed to make the best of our condition. In prayer we should first petition for strength to face our situation.

The Lord expects us to call upon Him during our times of trouble. We should then pray for relief and even for the removal of our obstacles. The Savior, in His most agonizing moments, petitioned: "Father, if thou be willing, remove this cup from me: nevertheless not my will, but thine be done" (Luke 22:42). It is most important that we too pray for and be willing to accept the will of our Father in Heaven. We are counseled to study the scriptures for answers to our suffering. We should remember that if we "Search diligently, pray always, and be believing, . . . all things shall work together for [our] good. . ." (D&C 90:24). We should seek the Spirit to be with us. The Holy Ghost will not only comfort us in our time of need but will ". . . show unto [us] all things what [we] should do" (2 Nephi 32:5). He will provide answers and increase our understanding. The Spirit will sustain us through our suffering.

We have the promise of the Lord that if we endure these things well, we can have *relief* from our suffering, and eternal *rewards* will be received. The Lord promised, "I will also ease the burdens which are put on your shoulders. . . I, the Lord God, do visit my people in their afflictions" (Mosiah 24:14). Our rewards will be great as we have the promise that "he that is faithful in tribulation, the reward of the same is greater in the kingdom of heaven" (D&C 58:2). This is a marvelous promise, for in the eternal perspective, we can never lose in our earthly adversities as long as we remain faithful through those tribulations. Experiences and opportunities that seem to be lost as a result of our earthly afflictions will be to our advantage in eternity. Heavenly Father will provide more than an adequate replacement for those things that we lose in our earthly experiences. We have the same promise that the Lord gave to the Prophet Joseph Smith when He said, "if thou endure it well, God shall exalt thee on high. . ." (D&C 121:8). There can be no greater blessing given to man than to be exalted.

Personal Perseverance 12

"... let us run with patience the race that is set before us." —(Hebrews 12:1)

Sometimes we are not successful in accomplishing our goals. The fault is not necessarily in our aspirations, in our attitudes, or in the actions that we take. Often, we do not have the strength, the stamina, or the steadfastness to endure to the end.

The principle of perseverance is critical to our success and may be the difference in our eternal destiny. If we fail to endure to the end, we may have to settle for a telestial estate with continued turmoil and torment, or for a terrestrial estate with its toil and tears, rather than a celestial condition with its possibilities of creation and of communication with Deity.

The rewards are great for all who are faithful to the finish, as they have the promise: "he that endureth to the end shall be saved" (Matthew 10:22). The promise is again given, "thou shalt be saved in the kingdom of God, which is the greatest of all the gifts of God. . ." (D&C 6:13). It is the faithful who will be given "all thrones and dominions, principalities and powers. . ." (D&C 121:29).

The steps to success have been given with their associated principles. If we practice these principles, we have the promise that our performance will become more perfect, and we will be successful. As the Lord has said, "I give unto you directions how you may act before me . . . I, the Lord am bound when ye do what I say . . ." (D&C 82:9-10).

It is important that we understand these principles and follow the great example of those who have practiced them to a high degree of perfection. The Savior and the living prophet should always be the ones we pattern our lives after. We must gain a full understanding of our purpose in life and set goals as did the Savior. Our commitment should be as complete as was Nephi's. We must have the confidence of David and Gideon, and the positive attitude of Nephi. Our relationships with others should be developed in a righteous manner as were those of Joseph, the son of Jacob. Our obedience should be observed like that of Adam and Abraham. We should emulate the motivation of the Master and have the willingness to work as did Moses and Jacob. Our adversities should be faced with the patience of Job using the Savior as an example for surviving our suffering.

If we properly follow these great examples of success, our challenge should be that when we near the end of our mission on earth, we will be able to say as Paul said, "I have fought a good fight, I have finished my course, I have kept the faith" (2 Timothy 4:7). Our challenge is to be able to answer as King Benjamin answered to his people, with "a clear conscience before God. . ." (Mosiah 2:27). Finally, we have the challenge to be able to respond as the Savior responded to Heavenly Father, "I have finished the work which thou gavest me to do" (John 17:4).

My challenge to you is the same as that of King Benjamin, "and now, if you believe all these things see that ye do them" (Mosiah 4:10). When we do these things, we will have the promise of Joshua that "thou shalt have good success" (Joshua 1:8).